More praise for

# BREAKING HATE

"A rare, exquisitely narrated tale of journeys to the edge and back, *Breaking Hate* illuminates a creeping danger that threatens to polarize American society and split it apart. It documents Christian Picciolini's inspired efforts to turn back a tide of hate about to engulf us all. A must-read for anyone who cares to understand what feeds violent extremism, and how it can be countered."

> —Dr. Arie Kruglanski, Distinguished Professor of Psychology at the University of Maryland and author of *The Three Pillars of Radicalization*

"Those who ignore Picciolini's agonizing and dire warnings about the pervasive and systematic alt-right movement, do so at all of our peril. We must instead listen intently to what he is telling us and internalize his poignantly told personal story and fervent efforts to repair fractured souls lost to forces beyond their control. Our survival as a civil society may depend upon it."

> —Glenn Frank, coauthor of *From Broken Glass: Surviving Hitler's Death Camps to Inspire a New Generation*

"At a time when the bonds of multiracial democracy and pluralism are being torn by political strife, growing hate group activity, and acts of white-supremacist terrorism, Christian Picciolini provides us a roadmap to a new sense of community and justice. As a former extremist himself, Picciolini knows what turns people into ticking time bombs and what it takes to defuse them; and more to the point, what it takes to prevent still more fuses from being lit. In *Breaking Hate*, he combines a keen sense of history with human psychology, sharp storytelling and the kind of hopefulness it will take to emerge from our current moment a healthier and more just nation. In this impressive volume he provides a critical glimpse inside the broken humanity of not only individual extremists, but the brokenness of America itself."

—Tim Wise, author of *White Like Me: Reflections on Race from a Privileged Son*

"With piercing insight and unrivaled compassion, *Breaking Hate* tells the tragic story of how extremism has torn our communities asunder and how every American can work together to end the epidemic of violence that has taken so many of our loved ones. In a country where more than 96 percent of mass shootings are perpetrated by men, we need to find ways of helping our boys grow into healthy young men who not only reject hate but also feel they have paths forward in today's economy."

—Andrew Yang, Democratic presidential candidate

# BREAKING HATE

ALSO BY CHRISTIAN PICCIOLINI

*White American Youth: My Descent into America's Most Violent Hate Movement—and How I Got Out*

# BREAKING HATE

## CONFRONTING THE
## NEW CULTURE OF EXTREMISM

## CHRISTIAN PICCIOLINI

BOOKS

NEW YORK   BOSTON

Hachette Books
Hachette Book Group
1290 Avenue of the Americas
New York, NY 10104
hachettebookgroup.com
twitter.com/hachettebooks

First Edition: February 2020

Hachette Books is a division of Hachette Book Group, Inc.
The Hachette Books name and logo are trademarks of Hachette Book Group, Inc.

The publisher is not responsible for websites (or their content) that are not owned by the publisher.

Christian Picciolini is available for select speaking engagements and press/media opportunities. To inquire, please email pr@picciolini.com or visit www.christianpicciolini.com.

Print book interior design by Six Red Marbles.

Library of Congress Cataloging-in-Publication Data has been applied for.

ISBNs: 978-0-316-52293-9 (hardcover), 978-0-316-52295-3 (ebook)

Printed in the United States of America

LSC-C

10 9 8 7 6 5 4 3 2 1

*For Britton, my boys, and Buddy,*
*who have lived these pages with me in magical ways*
*for the last thirty-odd years—*
*and always with love*

# Contents

## PART TWO

## Radical—"The True Believer"

## PART THREE

## De-Radicalization—"The Enlightened Seeker"

# Author's Note

The people, histories, and situations described in this book are based on real accounts of my work and life. I have, however, changed most names and identifying details of the individual stories and omitted, condensed, and reordered certain time lines. I have also re-created scenes where I was not present, based on the accounts of those involved. What I have not changed are any specific dates, general scenarios, or my intervention approaches.

Certain names—some which you may recognize—remain unchanged. These individuals have deliberately chosen hate and the public spotlight over the public good. As I believe sunlight is the best disinfectant, I leave them unmasked for transparency and, hopefully, their accountability. They know I am a beacon that won't go dark, should they ever decide to seek refuge from the storms they have created.

Cited as footnotes are some studies and statistics, though it would have been impossible to credit all the excellent researchers, analysts, mental health professionals, academics, writers, journalists, watchdogs, and first responders in the field who have shaped my understanding of violence-based extremism over the last thirty years. I also want to acknowledge those who directly inspired this book: the victims of hate and bias-based crimes, and the former extremists—"formers"—I have helped disengage from hate. I know the latter recognize their privilege in receiving a second chance and hope to make the most of it. For those in America's minority communities, who often do less damaging things than I've ever done, I stand with you—I see you and acknowledge the prejudice and the imbalance of justice you endure. I hope to raise your voices here, too.

I am not a licensed psychologist, social worker, faith healer, guru, or saint, but I base the concepts, theories, and approaches outlined in these pages on my thirty years of immersion and intensive effort in a space that, because of its ugly, covert, and dangerous nature, has been difficult to study—especially for outsiders. You'll soon learn I am a former violent extremist, who as a young man spent almost a decade during the 1980s and '90s as a leader in the American white-supremacist movement. Since denouncing racism, I have dedicated my life to ensuring others don't tread the same dark path I once did. I hope the insight I've gained while breaking free from hate—and as I continue to repair the harm I once caused—is a worthy complement to the important work of my professional peers and a useful road map to help others escape the darkness of extremism.

Christian Picciolini
*April 20, 2019*
*Chicago, Illinois, USA*

# Foreword

## By Malcolm Nance

On the morning of April 19, 1995, a young US Army veteran drove a Ryder truck filled with 4,500 pounds of improvised explosives made from ammonium nitrate fertilizer and high-octane racing car fuel to Oklahoma City, Oklahoma. He calmly parked the truck in front of the Alfred P. Murrah federal building and lit the fuse. Weeks before, Timothy McVeigh had done the same thing in a dry run. That time, he walked up the steps into the building and past the childcare center full of children belonging to federal workers. He found the FBI office on an upper floor at the rear of the building and went home to adjust his explosive payload. When he decided to carry out the plan, McVeigh arrived knowing that the first victims were going to be the children in the childcare center...and he did not care.

McVeigh was to become the most notorious American terrorist in our nation's history. A decorated combat veteran transformed into a racist killing machine when he made a conscious choice to build the bomb and kill as many of his fellow citizens as possible, but he was not always that way. He became radicalized through a book, a right-wing extremist blood fantasy called *The Turner Diaries*. The premise of the book was that an extremist white underground existed in the federal government and armed forces. They conspired to rid America of all other races and Jews. On the right signal, they would rise, steal the government's arms, and start a race war to cleanse America. That sign was the car bombing of the FBI headquarters in Washington, DC.

McVeigh and his fellow coconspirators, Terry Nichols, Michael Fortier, and his wife Lori decided they would start this race war. Timothy McVeigh was not the first extremist in American history radicalized by an obscure doctrine that believed in the superiority of the white race. Today, many Americans have taken up the call to mimic Nazi ideology, embrace the white-power movement, or ride on the coattails of racist southern secessionist recidivism. But McVeigh would be the one who put it into action.

Christian Picciolini was one of those who once heard the siren's call and became drawn to this violent extremist movement. A member of the white-power movement for nearly a decade, and as the leader of the Chicago Area Skinheads (CASH), he became seduced by a strident affirmation that the white race was the victim in America. He formed white-power music groups who espoused that diversity and the strength of character by a man or woman who was not of the white race was akin to chiseling the foundation for an all-white America. He, like many other Americans, found new meaning in the words and actions of Adolf Hitler and the Nazis. Christian put his radical beliefs to a new form of political propaganda music called "hate rock." With it, he brought in thousands of new followers. Yet, he would eventually come to question himself and seek to break away from the hatred.

*Breaking Hate* is a groundbreaking book. It reveals the depths of the modern white-power extremist movement and illustrates how easily the children of good-hearted, proud Americans can become transformed and corrupted by the dark-hearted hatred of the alt-right and white nationalism. Christian now helps others leave violent and racist campaigns, and helps them find their true heart and avert their eyes away from the darkness consuming their souls. He illustrates this through the stories of those who he has helped break free of the barrier of hatred they built around themselves.

*Breaking Hate* is a sorrowfully necessary book for the dark period America has found itself in the age of their openly racist champion, President Donald Trump. Reading these stories gives a poignant understanding of how law enforcement, government, or the average citizen have let go for too long the potential terrorists operating openly in our midst.

When Timothy McVeigh detonated his truck bomb, he knew the entire building would collapse on that childcare center and kill the children—black, white, brown, and Asian. He and other extremists seek to destroy the strength of America by attacking its diversity. This is where they are wrong, and this book will help you understand why we must defeat their every effort to grow and radicalize others. Timothy McVeigh killed nineteen babies in the childcare center and 149 other innocent Americans, but white-power terrorism has only made us embrace more fervently America's promise of "E Pluribus Unum"— *From Many, One.*

Malcolm Nance
*Hudson, New York*

# Introduction

---

# Nation of Hate

For over five hundred years, the blood of countless victims has stained the hands of "proud" and "patriotic" white supremacists and seeped into the rich soil we call the United States.

It began with Christopher Columbus in 1492. Upon sailing into the New World with three ships full of seaworn European mercenaries, Columbus and his "explorers" decimated the lives of the indigenous people and their tender-aged children—often raping them before selling them in overseas slave markets. The brutal dehumanization of nonwhites by white Europeans escalated with the broader colonization of the Americas from the fifteenth to the nineteenth century. Ten million natives and Africans died in the booming new transatlantic slave trade and the smallpox epidemic, which Columbus also introduced. Since then, the horrors of white supremacy on American soil have continued to manifest in insidious and grotesque ways.

Fast-forward to 1915: Hollywood's first blockbuster, *The Birth of a Nation,* debuted in nickelodeons across the United States as the country's first feature-length motion picture and the first movie ever screened inside the White House. Originally billed as *The Clansman,* the silent black-and-white drama depicts the Ku Klux Klan (KKK)—our nation's oldest and deadliest terror group—as heroic American patriots defending white Western values. The roaring prominence of the film inspired a Klan renaissance, and exploded national membership in the KKK's Invisible

Empire to four million by 1925—roughly 15 percent of the white US population at the time.

Despite any progress modern America has made in addressing the injustices of our forebears, we have never escaped the shadow of white supremacy. Slavery became black disenfranchisement under Jim Crow laws, and Jim Crow morphed into the less recognizable—but still ravaging—racist policies in our institutions of financial lending, housing, education, and criminal justice. Tragically, this corrupt narrative still remains the unchallenged legacy of our United States.

Racist embers were again stoked during the 2016 presidential campaign and the subsequent election of Donald J. Trump as the forty-fifth president of the United States. President Trump's embodiment of an autocratic strongman and his use of divisive "identity politics" and fear rhetoric long espoused by bigots—as well as immigration policies that appear inspired by Columbus himself—fueled a new generation of American hate.

Wielding executive power like a medieval battering ram, Trump's polemics against undocumented immigrants and minority groups fanned the flames of racist vitriol to rally an aggrieved political base, body-slamming an already wounded nation. His Twitter platform became a megaphone to tens of millions of disaffected white Americans, where he scapegoated their afflictions and irrational fears upon nonwhites, non-Christians, women, the mainstream news media, and progressives, while funneling their outrage into votes at the ballot box. Hot-button wedge issues, including immigration reform, religion, social welfare, reproductive rights, gender, government corruption, gun laws, and the use of presidential privilege, duped Americans into cosigning his crooked agenda to "drain the swamp" of DC bureaucracy. Trump further amplified fear levels with "shit-hole country" statements about friendly nations and rants targeting the "lying" media, while also promoting white genocide conspiracies and reckless birther lies that painted his predecessor as an illegitimate president who'd been born in Kenya.

Since the 2016 election, the continued breakdown of discourse has made it impossible to reach a national consensus on how to address these critical social and political moments. Hindered by disruptive foreign influence campaigns and the disturbing and very real proliferation of "fake news" that is meant to influence and divide Americans, we have yet to understand what the lasting implications will be for our fragile democracy.

The growing heft of information we consume makes defining the problem even more difficult. Feeding our internal insecurities and triggering our sensitivities, Internet memes, social media platforms, political podcasts, disinformation crafted to masquerade as authentic web ads, college campus propaganda, and online "fringe" forums have become fodder for a new era of ideological warfare. Preparation for this war is taking place not just online, but also in prison yards, around office watercoolers, on cable "news" networks, and among our children while they play multiplayer video games (it's not the violent game content we need to fear).

Until recently, most Americans enjoyed the privilege of living near the center of the political spectrum, only inching toward a precipice when an issue hit home. In today's America, however, we've become forced to choose between limited one-size-fits-all options intent on herding us toward opposing cliffs to leap from. What was once a fissure between value systems has widened into a Grand Canyon of ideological difference and primed America for the fires of violent extremism to ignite—and Donald Trump's incendiary "America First" platform lit the fuse.

From the ashes of old-fashioned American white supremacy, a new social carcinogen has emerged. The rapid growth of the racist "alt-right" movement and a new strain of white-supremacist ideology that calls itself "white nationalism" are making hate the most dangerous contagion in America again—and we've reached epidemic levels.

The ugly and tragic events of August 11 and 12, 2017, in Charlottesville, Virginia, bear witness to this alarming trend. Hundreds of white nationalists from across the United States descended on Charlottesville to stage a series of public rallies, painting themselves as a conservative grassroots effort to "Unite the Right." Claiming to protest the removal of Confederate monuments, the bloody endeavor was instead a bullhorn to alert a "friendly" president that white supremacy was alive and thriving in America under his watch.

Clean-cut, young white men dressed in khakis and polo shirts adorned with Nazi insignia gathered in the blistering Virginia heat, carrying flaming torches and battle flags. United in their collective paranoia that the white race is facing cultural genocide, they clutched defaced placards proclaiming, "It's OK to be White" and "White Lives Matter." In unabashed unison, they chanted, "Blood and soil!" on ground where their European ancestors once spilled the blood of people of color.

Violent clashes between hordes of white supremacists holding makeshift shields and an army of counterprotesters ensued, and yet again, senseless racist violence would claim another victim. Killed by a neo-Nazi marcher who rammed his vehicle at full speed into a crowd of anti-racist activists leaving the demonstration, Heather Heyer was a young woman entering the prime of her life. After deciding her silence was no longer acceptable in the face of such hatred, Heather protested the rallies and sacrificed her precious life for her values. Heather's mother, my dear friend Susan Bro, stated at her daughter's memorial service, "They tried to kill my child to shut her up. Well, guess what? You just magnified her." Indeed they did.

But what actual progress have we made in preventing white-supremacist violence since it cut Heather Heyer's life so tragically short? Not much. In fact, things have gotten worse.

Since Heather's death in Charlottesville in 2017, violent white supremacists have killed and injured many more innocent victims. Emboldened by a commander in chief—whom notorious white nationalists have publicly stated supports their vision of making America white again—white extremists are committing acts of racially and politically motivated violence in record numbers. One only needs to turn on cable news to find horrific stories of journalists and politicians targeted by pipe bombs, schoolchildren assassinated by classmates, and the faithful slaughtered inside their houses of worship.

In 2017, the FBI reported that seven thousand hate crimes were documented in the United States the previous year.* The number itself is staggering, but considering that many hate crimes go unreported by law enforcement agencies due to the difficulty in classifying and prosecuting them, it is even more so. The Anti-Defamation League (ADL) published a similarly chilling report in 2019, concluding that incidents of American far-right violence had accounted for almost all hate-related murders in 2018.† But this isn't just America's problem anymore.

On March 15, 2019, soon after the ADL released its report, an Australian white supremacist attacked two New Zealand mosques with an assortment of loaded semiautomatic assault weapons. Through a Facebook live stream, the world watched as the terrorist massacred fifty-one peaceful Muslim worshippers—men, women, and small children. The killer wore identifiable white-nationalist movement markings on his body armor (insignia supporting a deadly neo-Nazi militia in Ukraine) and left behind a revealing manifesto, providing further proof of a growing transnational terror network. Just five months later, a similar tragedy played out when an anti-immigrant gunman killed twenty-two people in a Walmart in El Paso, Texas. The shooter's manifesto cited the New Zealand attacks as inspiration.

To keep this deadly trend of violent extremism from spiraling out of control, it is imperative that we examine it carefully—and from deep within.

Extremism, regardless of whether it's motivated by a political, religious, or social doctrine, flourishes when a critical mass of people believe their lives are becoming meaningless, displaced, or disempowered. Extremists feast on frenzy and polarization during times of crisis. Fear is primary sustenance for extremism to thrive, and its survival rests on the ability to foment the chaotic conditions that keeps us broken and afraid. The

---

* *Hate Crime Statistics, 2017* (Washington, DC: Federal Bureau of Investigation, 2018).
† *Murder and Extremism in the United States in 2018* (New York: Anti-Defamation League, 2019).

strategy is simple: turn everyday victims into perpetrators of "rough justice" by trading them a "great cause" for their discontent, while fooling them into believing they're still victims.

When faced with losing something of great value or importance—one can think of the disappearing middle class or the hollowed-out job market in economically challenged American communities such as the Rust Belt—desperate people tend to seek out radical solutions for their mounting grievances. Even if frustrations stem from necessary social or economic equalization, the threat of marginalization—or "replacement"—can lead to intense fear, and the sudden downturn mistaken for oppression.

Today, more than ever, ideologues at the furthest edges of the political spectrum are using crisis to bait aggrieved, isolated, even privileged and willfully ignorant Americans with glory-driven promises as a panacea for their woes.

Extremists use deceptive online marketing tactics and spin elaborate conspiracy theories to lure fresh recruits—mostly male, young, intelligent, middle-class, idealistic, disenchanted, and alienated. Narratives are crafted to feed distrust and antipathy toward the mainstream. Efforts become amplified through the dangerous hyperbole and paranoia infused from our highest seats of power (as well as by our personal blind spots and unconscious biases). Our deeply fractured sociopolitical environment and collective distress have also emboldened hostile foreign actors to target our open wounds and inject their poison into our bloodstream.

Still, even as the delicate fibers of America's fabric are being ripped to shreds by extremism, there are some people who claim the threat of violent white supremacy is a "hoax."

The sliver of pessimism still lodged in me from my former life as an extremist agrees that as a society we are sliding headfirst into Mahatma Gandhi's warning of "an eye for an eye leaves the whole world blind." While that may be how we're trending, I refuse to believe surrendering our nation over to hate is the only remaining option. Instead, I follow the wisdom of Malcolm X: "Sometimes you have to pick the gun up to put the gun down." I know this sounds backward and counterintuitive.

To be clear, except in self-defense or to protect others, I don't condone violence. The "weapon" I now hold is one whose barrel I have stared down from both sides: hate. My ammunition is the objective truth that radical ideologies are not what lead people to these destructive movements. No one is born to hate. I have found this bit of rare insight to be more powerful than any weapon Smith & Wesson can forge.

For those who align themselves with extremist ideologies, doctrine is but the final component that locks into place. Radical ideologies and extremist movements act like green traffic lights, signaling to those who have "stalled" in life where to direct blame for their grievances, anger, and insecurities—sometimes in violent ways—instead of working to resolve their obstacles in a positive or healthy manner. Feeling newly empowered, the cruelty that extremists adopt is the fraudulent license that grants them permission to project their pain onto others.

I've learned the only way to break this cycle of hate we are stuck in is to not distance ourselves from the problem, but to invest in one another, and in our failing "human infrastructure."

Instead of attacking racists for their ignorance, I draw them in closer, knowing that beneath their protective armor of hate is a fractured human who is wearing it to mask their agony, shame, and fear.

If we can acknowledge that underlying environmental, emotional, and/or physical challenges, or *any* multitude of challenging life factors, are what give people their first push toward extremism—and not the other way around—then hope exists of diverting future generations from its devastating path altogether, and redemption is possible for those still wandering lost.

To confront this new culture of extremism that is emerging in America, we must approach it holistically just as the great Jewish scientist Dr. Jonas Salk tackled the epidemic of polio: treat the sick while inoculating others against contracting the disease. Although my work intervening with violent extremists is one way to "treat the sick," the information I offer in these pages illustrates how anyone—at home, in the classroom, around the dinner table, in a legislative body, even one-on-one in public (with caution)—can intervene to prevent future generations from succumbing to extremism.

We can avert many of the tragedies we've become forced to accept as convention if we acknowledge that we are all "broken" and imperfect and that no one is alone in their despair. It's something we all share. This universal brokenness is at the very core of the human condition, and it is the fundamental glue that can put us back together.

Yet, to fully eradicate hate, we must also heal the lingering wounds of our nation's past failures. We must acknowledge the grave errors we've made and learn from them, while also learning from one another, calling out hate by its name, and enlisting those harmed by it to shape our future together. Let's embrace the values of our great democracy—but understand we have much to do to fulfill its potential. Pledge allegiance to one another and the rest of humanity, using our shared bond of imperfection to grow and make our nation a bastion of courage and freedom. Only then will we embody the strength and idealism we have long professed.

Our *greatness* still lies ahead—but only our *goodness* will lead us there.

America—this is your intervention.

# Prologue

---

# The Crossroads of Union and Division

I SPENT THE SUMMER OF 1987 shadowboxing my teenage demons, buzzed on a steady diet of cheap beer and bitter-tasting ditch weed—two substances I hoped would become easier to score when I started high school in three months.

On Friday nights in Blue Island, Illinois, the center of my universe became whichever garage I decided to lean against in the dead-end alley behind the corner of Union and Division Streets, a block downwind from the weekly fish fry in the basement of Saint Donatus Church. My *nonna*—the Italian grandmother who practically raised me—dragged me to Mass there every Sunday, making me kneel, sit, and stand so many goddamn times I could only pray to God to please make it stop.

I jumped ship on the Holy Spirit at the end of eighth grade when my parents moved us from the suburbs back to Blue Island on the southwest side of Chicago. After ditching the halls of my Catholic elementary school, I decided I wouldn't be anyone's faithful servant anymore. I grew up that summer, and not just physically—in addition to sprouting hair on my chin and my chest all of me got older, wiser. When I got to my new neighborhood, carving a path to escape my family's shadow became paramount to my existence. I assured myself this would be the year I'd make real friends and everything would change for me. I could feel it in my new, stocky bones.

Blue Island was the working-class, mostly Italian neighborhood on the edge of the city where my parents lived before I was born; where my grandparents now raised me while my mom and dad worked in their beauty shop around the clock. Buddy, my four-year-old baby brother, needed relatives to look after him when my mother went back to work styling hair, my parents claimed, and that's why they needed to move back near my grandparents. I knew my mom and dad were lying; it was because the shop wasn't doing well and they were going broke. I figured poverty wouldn't be half as bad as being almost fourteen and only having my kid brother to hang out with.

"This is some shitty ditch weed, dude," I said to Scully—one of the neighborhood burnouts—on a muggy, otherwise uneventful August night. Scully was a year older than me, though we'd both be first-year high school students in the fall. His long, curly auburn hair fell around his shoulders, framing pimple-covered cheeks as red and bright as his Michael Jordan jersey. He wore that Chicago Bulls jersey every day, even though it was two sizes too big for his gangly frame and hung past his shorts. Scully got held back in fifth grade for kicking his gym teacher in the nuts for making fun of his freckles, so I wasn't going to be the one to tell him his jersey looked like a dress—even if we weren't smoking his weed.

My fingertips burned on the last few pulls from the joint as my buzz kicked in. Scully had copped it for five bucks from bow-legged Jimmy Beausoleil at the old abandoned train bridge before the police hassled them for underage drinking. In exchange for their case of Miller High Life, the cops let them go with a warning—again. They hadn't found the weed and wouldn't be back until they wanted to drink on the job for free or flirt with the high school girls who drank there after Friday-night football games.

As I turned to pass the roach to Scully, a thunderous roar punched a hole in the dense night air. Two bright columns of light and the nose of a rumbling muscle car tore through the alley toward us. Emerging from the pale glow of a giant dust cloud, the black firebird bounced over the rough backstreet and skidded to a stop in front of me, kicking up bits of gravel that stung my face like raining hail.

I stood frozen, realizing Scully was long gone.

The door of the iron beast groaned open, and a thin, fair-skinned man at least twice my age stepped out. He looked worn, like a mercenary back from war. The flickering lamppost overhead was enough for me to catch glints of beaded sweat resting atop his clean-shaven scalp and flashes of his stubbled and determined face. As the man advanced toward me, crossing through streams of headlight, I fixated on his tall, black combat boots. Time seemed to slow as brilliant glimmers of amber light bounced off their shiny leather surface. Before I could process what was happening, he closed the distance between us and in one swift motion—like if Bruce Lee were a bald white ninja—smacked the side of my head with one hand and snatched the tiny joint from my fingers with the other, dropping it to the ground and crushing it with the heel of his steel-toed boot.

I wasn't sure whether to be more upset about losing the last of the weed or that I was about to get my ass kicked.

It was too late to run. The bald man's hand was already on my shoulder.

He leaned in, aimed his intense slate eyes into mine, and spoke with purpose: "Communists and Jews want promising, young white men like you to get hooked on these nasty drugs so you're kept docile through your own genocide. Did you know that?"

I did not.

I hadn't ever met a Jewish person. I knew the priests at school didn't think much of them, Jews having apparently crucified their Lord and Savior, Jesus Christ. But communists were a different story. Even at almost fourteen, I knew they were the bad guys. Why else would my boyhood idol Rocky Balboa knock the snot out of a Russian commie in the greatest "Italian" film of all time? The man's other words—*docile, genocide*—were so foreign to me I could only assume he knew what he was talking about.

"Tell me your name, son." He straightened up and spoke in a fatherly tone, his voice sounding like he'd swallowed fragments of the fractured pavement beneath my trembling legs. Mocked throughout my childhood for having a surname that could be rhymed however unfortunately with *weenie*, I was afraid to tell him. Worse, if he caught even a whiff that I was the weird foreign kid everyone picked on for bringing Nutella sandwiches to school for lunch, he'd pound me into minced meat. With no meaningful friendships and zero protection against bullies, I was an easy target—something I'd become used to by then. There was no chance of this encounter ending well for me.

Bracing myself, I let out a lukewarm: "Chris…Picciolini." The instant jab I expected from the imposing bald man in boots never came.

He instead paused for a moment and gave me a friendly pat on the back before letting his arm fall at his side. "Italian!" he proclaimed. I kept my body clenched in case he was planning a surprise attack.

"Yeah. My parents are from Italy, so what?" My eyes darted around the alley, studying it for getaway options and coming up empty. The only escape was hopping a fence at least eight feet off the ground, far higher than I could reach even with a good jump and a running start. "But I'm American," I replied.

"Now Rome, that was once a glorious empire!" he said. "Roman women are one of God's most exquisite creations." He rested his hand on my shoulder again, gripping it like an old friend.

"Um…hmm, yeah," I muttered, confused by his reaction but relieved I wouldn't have to explain another shiner from bullies to my parents.

The bald man continued to ask me questions as we stood there talking for twenty minutes. Having no close friends, my world consisted of parents who worked ninety-hour weeks and grandparents who were too old to connect with their teenage grandson. It seemed twenty minutes longer than anyone had ever engaged me in my entire life.

So, I listened.

He regaled me with tales of the rise of the Holy Roman Empire and the fall of Constantinople, the Battle of Carthage, and other European conquests and civilizations—all of which he described as "glorious."

Explaining the impact that "white men" made throughout the annals of world history, he illustrated in great detail how America would be a third-world country if it weren't for the "boldness of whiteness."

A freight train roared over the tracks behind us, unleashing a loud, repeating thud. I jumped. In my nervous state, intrigued by the man's attention and overwhelmed by the concepts he had unfurled before me, it sounded like a tommy gun.

The man laughed. "There's a lot to be afraid of in this world, son," he said, nodding at the train, "but that old locomotive ain't one of them." Inaction, he claimed, was what I needed to fear. He stressed how mighty cultures of the past had faded into oblivion because of their ambivalence toward conquering what he described as an invasion by "lesser" civilizations. It was, he cautioned, a tale of the tragic consequences suffered by white nations throughout history that hadn't fought for their survival.

After offering me a Marlboro from the crumpled pack of cigarettes tucked under his T-shirt sleeve, he told me about how white civilizations around the world were under attack by the "globalist agendas of the Washington capitalists," and that if I cared for my future I needed to stand up to stop this "cultural massacre" from happening. Once I figured out he wasn't talking about a secret plot by the professional hockey team in DC, his wisdom sank in, and it wasn't long before I became hooked on the worldview he revealed to me.

For twenty short minutes—a lifetime to me as a teen—the bald man in tall, black combat boots stayed with me in that stinking alley, connecting with me until I felt important and respected. Knowing I felt undervalued, he told me I mattered. It was the first time in my young life that I felt someone—anyone—saw me.

Clark Martell, America's first neo-Nazi skinhead leader, then extended his right arm in a stiff Roman salute and welcomed a barely teenage me into his burgeoning new white-power skinhead movement. I had just become one of its earliest and youngest members; I just didn't know it yet.

No one saw my radicalization to extremism coming. Not my parents, grandparents, my teachers, or the gang of teenage bruisers who made my life hell growing up. I didn't even know what happened at first. When I unveiled my new radical persona as a white-power skinhead, the people around me were shocked and horrified, scrambling to make sense of it—but by then, it was too late. I had forged my frustrations into a weapon to use against them, digging in and doubling down to show them they had failed and abandoned me and that I was better off without them.

Following that fateful meeting in the dead-end alley at the crossroads of Union and Division, I allowed myself to forget I'd been born into a decent, hardworking, Italian American *immigrant* family. I dove headfirst into America's racist underground, empowered by the offers of camaraderie and meaning—and I traded obscurity for hate, making it the currency that ruled my life for almost a decade.

Adapting to this new world was thrilling at first. The more I absorbed what Martell and his crew of older skinheads told me, the easier it became to justify the violence that accompanied my new beliefs. It was everyone else, the willing "enemy combatants" of the world, who were the source of my angst and pain. And they deserved punishment for their crimes against me and the white race they were trying to annihilate, or so I believed.

Though I was hard-pressed to find any evidence of the "antiwhite" plots I feasted on and swallowed whole, I didn't hesitate to blame "shadowy Jews" and "secret globalist agendas" for "destroying" white civilization, or insinuate that "blacks" were responsible for all the crime, drugs, and violence in our cities. Socially conscious whites also became my enemy— "race traitors." Overlooking my brutality against people of color during that time, I became deaf and blind to generations of suffering endured by women and people in marginalized communities—many of whom still face the same injustices today. Believing immigrants were stealing jobs away from white Americans allowed me to betray the non-racist upbringing of my Italian parents, who were often the victims of prejudice as new immigrants, and who struggled to keep a small business alive with no outside help.

Convinced my fight was the good fight against a world conspiring to oppress me—a straight, white male—I was determined to emerge as the victor, whatever the cost.

In 1990, three years after my radicalization into extremism, I inherited Clark Martell's hate group—the Chicago Area Skinheads (CASH)—making me second in a notorious lineage the world eventually saw marching, albeit in tidier appearance, through the streets of Charlottesville in 2017. When Martell was sentenced to ten years in prison for one of the first hate crimes ever prosecuted in the United States, I took over running America's first neo-Nazi skinhead gang. By then, I was already recognized around Chicago as a vicious street brawler, and I was stockpiling illegal weapons and ammunition for what I believed was an imminent race war. I fronted one of the world's earliest white-power bands, and in 1992, we became the first American skinhead group to perform in Europe and spread our racist message through music—toxic propaganda I am still unable to scrub from the Internet decades later.

During my eight years in the American white-supremacist movement, I led a division of the violent Hammerskin Nation, a neo-Nazi group that almost became implicated in a plot to conspire with late Libyan dictator Muammar Gaddafi to ignite an armed revolt against American Jews. By sheer luck, the Canadian Security Intelligence Service intervened before my cell became involved, and the unlikely terror alliance between homegrown white extremists and radical jihadists overseas—against what they collectively view as "the Jewish problem"— didn't materialize, at least not yet.

I recited and honored the racist "Fourteen Words" mission statement that white supremacists cleave to their chests: *We must secure the existence of our people and a future for white children.* What I didn't know then was that instead of setting into motion the imaginary white utopia the pledge purported to guarantee, my actions in its pursuit did nothing but inflict senseless trauma on undeserving victims and their loved ones, including my own.

Many of my old comrades died. More went to prison. I carry this cautionary tale with me—along with the memories I can't erase—everywhere I go, and I share it, hoping it might help others see danger lurking ahead before they travel too far down the same damaging road I once walked alone. Though I was ashamed of my personal history at first, I shared it anyway because running from my past was the wrong thing to do. Now it brings me peace, knowing that when I discuss my story with someone who is disengaging from extremism, or if I bring it to a classroom, stage, or media interview, the knowledge I've gained through my painful mistakes and the intense self-reflection that followed now helps others change their lives for the better. My journey has been amazing, and I'm inspired every time I see light bulbs turn on when people finally understand how it's possible for someone to allow hate to eat them alive—but also find their way back to humanity.

One question almost everyone asks me: How did a young Christian Picciolini, a shy, "normal," and idealistic kid from Chicago, raised by a modest immigrant family, with no apparent bigoted influences, get so lost down the path to hate and extremism?

One word: *potholes.*

My journey through an otherwise privileged childhood was riddled with metaphorical potholes that widened and multiplied with time and neglect. Potholes are the unresolved traumas buried deep within us. These roadblocks can detour us or carjack us altogether if we're not careful—and they can keep us from discovering a more positive and life-affirming path.

My life as a teenager, like the lives of so many young Americans today, was an obstacle course of emotional and psychological land mines. The weighty uncertainty of not knowing who I was, where—if anywhere—I belonged, or what meaning my life held overwhelmed me, so I wandered aimless and uncertain.

I was desperate for healthy doses of *identity, community,* and *purpose* (ICP).* Had I discovered them in positive spaces, instead of through a skinhead on a grimy backstreet, my personal trajectory would have been much different.

The need to fulfill ICP is so essential, I have found the hunt for them to be a critical ingredient in the descent into extremism of every person I have worked with. Whether positive or destructive, ICP are the foundations one builds their core beliefs upon; decisions, actions, and behaviors all stem from their pursuit. Throughout my youth, I groped for them as if crawling through a thick fog with eyes wide shut. Without someone to help me decipher my ICP deficits, and to guide me responsibly around my potholes, I started alone on a dangerous and rocky trek into an alternative reality dominated by "us" versus "them" narratives, where everyone but myself was condemned as a threat to my existence and the future of civilization as I saw it.

Since leaving the white-power movement in 1996, I have obsessed over the questions of *how* and *why* I ended up radicalized into a life of hate and extremism, dissecting every folly from those squandered years. Understanding the motivations of my misguided youth became more critical in 2004 when my twenty-year-old brother, following in my destructive footsteps, lost his life to senseless gun violence on the streets of Chicago.

The intense self-evaluation that followed my brother's death forced me to confront the actions of my past. Dealing with what I had done head-on, I became driven by the notion that after so many grave personal errors, I could somehow help prevent the sickness I once spread from infecting others. It was all I could do to keep myself from

---

* *Author's note:* My theory's name, ICP, should not be confused with Insane Clown Posse, the white rap/hip-hop duo from Detroit, Michigan—although with a few minor tweaks, this book could very quickly describe their fanatical and "extreme" clown-makeup-wearing subculture. In 2011, the FBI classified the band's Juggalo supporters as a "loosely organized hybrid gang."

falling back into despair and finding false comfort down other dark pathways.

I am fortunate and privileged to have survived my painful ordeal, however scarred it left me to know that the harm I once caused could never fully be undone. It took years for me to accept it, but I could not ignore my responsibility to ensure my sinister legacy didn't repeat itself with others. This voluntary penance for my past sins is both the impetus and backbone of this book.

What I learned from my journey into and away from hate now helps me combat it. Today, the number of former extremists—"formers" as we're known in my circles—I have helped disengage from extremism is in the hundreds. From white lone-wolf terrorists and suit-and-tie campus Nazis to ISIS foreign fighters and would-be school shooters in America's heartland, with my guidance, they have navigated the unforgiving mountainous terrain back to humanity.

The return journey is never accomplished through heated ideological debate or argument. I don't use shame or physical force to change their minds. I don't bother paying anyone lip service, and I certainly don't bust lips anymore. I try not to tell people they're wrong—though having lived their mistakes I know, perhaps more than most, they are. And I avoid calling them *monsters*. I don't label them with anything demeaning, because I understand the negative implications of such dehumanizing tactics. Instead, I work hard to earn their trust, and I listen with empathy. Responding with equal parts cautious vulnerability and measured compassion, I help them uncover the truth about who they really are—keeping accountability for their misdeeds at the fore as the terms for their forgiveness going forward. What often moves me is not what people say but instead the pain, trauma, and uncertainty they say little about or that no words can describe.

I filter out the deafening white noise of ideology, ignoring it to focus on which underlying motivations detoured them to those wrong conclusions—and I discover which potholes still exist.

Then I become a pothole filler.

Contrary to how extremists win the hearts and minds of unsuspecting "marginalized seekers"—passionate but vulnerable idealists like I was at fourteen—by manipulating their hopes and fears; I win back those frightened hearts and manipulated minds through empathy, humanization, and reflection. My goal is to send them off into the world as "enlightened seekers," equipped to repair the harm they caused.

Nothing worth pursuing comes easy. The process known as *de-radicalization*—disengaging from a violence-driven political or religious extremist ideology—is complex and requires a careful approach. Because ideology is often used as convenient reasoning to project pain—pain that requires confronting—it is much easier to radicalize a person than it is to bring them back. But rest assured, positive change can occur in even the most "lost" of causes and redemption *is* possible. It just doesn't happen overnight, and the immense rebuilding it requires is raw and sometimes painful.

As outsiders, learning to *see the child, not the monster*—regardless of whether the individual is sixteen or sixty years old—is essential to understanding how we can end this vicious cycle of hate. Empathy for a racist does not mean appeasement of their hateful beliefs nor equate to an endorsement of criminal or violent behavior. People *must* be accountable for their actions—I've held myself to task and continue doing so. But I also know that receiving unexpected (and often unwarranted) compassion from someone we might not otherwise show to ourselves is the *only* thing I've ever seen truly break hate. It's never simple or comfortable, but it's a wonder to witness every time it occurs.

Through a series of interwoven vignettes, we'll venture into the dark world of extremism and examine the phenomena of radicalization and de-radicalization. By examining the lives of some of those hoping to escape hate for a brighter future, and we'll witness how even in the most troubling of circumstances change *is* possible. It is thanks to these essential stories that I can guide you through the intimate process of extremist disengagement.

Hate is real, and the stakes of eradicating it from our society are existential. Ambivalence only perpetuates hate's toxicity and widens our fractures. Let's instead harness our ability to amplify the goodness in one another and commit to being the antidote to hate.

We can persevere through this bleak period in our nation's history. This time, though, it is imperative we learn all it teaches us.

# BREAKING HATE

# PART ONE

# PRE-RADICALIZATION

## "The Marginalized Seeker"

*They hate because they fear, and they fear because they feel that the deepest feelings of their lives are being assaulted and outraged. And they do not know why; they are powerless pawns in a blind play of social forces.*

—Richard Wright, *Native Son*

*I imagine one of the reasons people cling to their hates so stubbornly is because they sense, once hate is gone, they will be forced to deal with pain.*

—James Baldwin, *The Fire Next Time*

# 1

---

## Warning Signs:
## The Prelude to Hate

### *Kassandra*

"SHE'S GONE, CHRISTIAN," Meredith sobbed.

The din of clanking flatware and midday chatter inside my favorite Chicago delicatessen made her words pulsing through my mobile phone hard to decipher. When Meredith's number popped up on my screen, it was always a crapshoot whether something horrible had happened—again. Miming to my colleague that I needed to step outside to take the call, I cupped a hand over my free ear and snaked through the scrum of hipsters and busboys at Manny's Deli and out the front door.

"Campus police called...they found Kassandra's phone in her dorm." Meredith's hurried words ebbed into staccato whimpers. "Jack is with me, and we're driving...to meet campus police...dear God."

"Meredith, please slow down." Rain speckled the cracked pavement around me. "Breathe. I can't understand you—say that again."

I already sensed whatever came out of Meredith's mouth next would mean one of two terrible things: yet another significant regression with her seventeen-year-old white-nationalist daughter, Kassandra, or worse, Kassandra's Nazi boyfriend followed through with what he long threatened and physically took her from her family. Neither scenario was good, but the latter would be devastating.

"Jakob abducted Kassandra," was all I heard before losing the rest of her words to the ether. The humid Chicago air squeezed the remaining breath out of me. Meredith's voice was flat with despair, empty and heavy like the fog rolling in from Lake Michigan. I lowered the phone and pressed it against my chest, the speaker vibrating my skin as she wept for her missing teenage daughter a thousand miles away. I shuddered, feeling responsible, as if my chronic fear of this moment had somehow manifested it.

My head spun as thoughts raced inside of it—and it all rushed back in a flash.

Like a tornado of binary fragments, a stream of digital evidence from my year-long investigation into Kassandra's online tormentors swirled in my mind—the suspects, aliases, accomplices, doctored videos, manipulated images, IP addresses, map coordinates, and countless screen grabs of bogus alt-right and pro-Trump social media accounts. Thousands of them all linked to Kassandra through a single nexus— Jakob Bergsson, her online Nazi boyfriend. Following the never-ending trail of rancid breadcrumbs to protect Kassandra and her family from Bergsson consumed me.

Now, she was gone.

It no longer mattered that I had made a solid identification on two suspects I believed were conspiring to lure Kassandra into thinking "Jakob Bergsson" was a real person: a Peruvian man living in Northern California named Santiago Amaro, and his partner, Maksim Volkov, a Russian millennial in Moscow, whom I labeled *Troll Zero*. As far as I could tell, the pair used the Jakob Bergsson fake-boyfriend alias to catfish at least four other underage female victims besides Kassandra. I warned the girls' families that an imposter boyfriend was grooming their young loved ones as white-supremacist mouthpieces but none responded to my phone messages or emails. The other girls likely shared revealing selfies like Kassandra had, and the looming threat of blackmail was also keeping them compliant.

The dizzying scenario made me question my sanity many times since meeting Kassandra. But I was damn sure of one thing: Jakob

Bergsson—the blond-haired, blue-eyed Aryan avatar Kassandra fell in love with over the Internet, the romantic twenty-three-year-old German American Nazi boy from Eagle, Idaho, who stole her heart and robbed her of her mind—did *not* exist in real life. He was a fraud.

The bizarre notion of a Russian Internet troll and a Latino immigrant living in Northern California conspiring to impersonate an American neo-Nazi was puzzling enough, but that they would go to such insane lengths for over eighteen months to dupe a random American teenager and her family gnawed at me. It was unlike any case of extremist radicalization I had encountered in almost twenty years of disengagement work, and I couldn't figure out why she was being targeted by these two discrete foreign men. *Sex trafficking? The Russian mob? A doomsday cult?* I wrestled with every possible warped scheme.

Jakob Bergsson—Kassandra's virtual boyfriend—was a self-anointed white supremacist, to be sure, but at least one of the real people behind the Bergsson alias appeared to be nonwhite and into non-movement-related cybercrimes like deep-web drug sales and financial pyramid schemes. The whole charade left me confused and in constant worry about Kassandra and her family's safety.

When I first discovered a connection between the Jakob Bergsson alias and thousands of fake pro-Trump social media accounts, I wondered if it was somehow related to the upcoming election before quickly whiffling it off as farfetched. Four months later, on January 6, 2017, when the CIA and FBI announced Russian president Vladimir Putin's intelligence directorate—the FSB—had meddled in and influenced the 2016 US presidential election in favor of Donald Trump, it confirmed my suspicions.*

How did Kassandra's radicalization fit into this? None of it made sense when I first stumbled on it. But as evidence piled up, a telling

---

* *Background to "Assessing Russian Activities and Intentions in Recent US Elections: The Analytic Process and Cyber Incident Attribution"* (Washington, DC: US Office of the Director of National Intelligence, 2017).

picture emerged. Still, my revelation to Kassandra and her family about the two men behind her fake boyfriend's social media accounts had failed to wake her from her nightmare.

*I am not losing my damn mind,* I convinced myself for the millionth time. Battling legions of doubt, along with a Russian troll brigade engaged in a furious siege on my will, took its toll on me. Bergsson had promised to come for Kassandra before, but the veiled threats never amounted to anything. This time, though, the elusive digital specter kept its word.

"Everything kosher?" my colleague asked as she approached me in the parking lot with an open umbrella and two bags of deli takeaway in tow. "I figured you got tangled up in that call, so I ordered us a couple of pastrami sandwiches to go."

My eyes lifted from their locked-downward stare, drops of dangling rain leaping from the brim of my cap. *I gave the FBI all my evidence on Jakob Bergsson. Why wouldn't they use it to stop him?* Eight months after I turned over evidence of Bergsson's social media scam to the feds, I was still pissed at them for not following up with me—and now Kassandra was missing.

I tried in vain to say some comforting words to Meredith on the other end of the line, but the truth was I was a mess, too. After gathering the details of her daughter's abduction, I said a clumsy goodbye and left her crying on the other end.

Sensing my distress, my colleague leaned in closer with her umbrella to shield me from the downpour I had somehow ignored. "You're soaked. Can I give you a ride somewhere?"

"Yeah," I replied, breaking my daze. "To the airport."

Most of my many interactions with ideological extremists over the years have not involved high-stakes abductions or international espionage, as young Kassandra's did. Still, neither of those frightening scenarios is much of a rarity in my workload these days either. Typically, these extremist disengagements—or *off-rampings*—begin with a concise but cautious appeal from an individual nearing their bottom, or, more commonly, a panicked or puzzled bystander—a loved one or acquaintance—who is worried that someone they care about has "suddenly" become lost to hate. Almost always, the frantic email, social media message, or phone text will include the same two vulnerable words: *Please help.*

In Kassandra's case, the desperate plea came to me from her father, Jack, a year before she went missing. On September 4—two months shy of the 2016 US presidential election—Jack and his wife, Meredith, discovered that their daughter Kassandra transitioned from the bright and shy girl they thought they knew into a neo-Nazi YouTube sensation.

> *My wife and I learned this morning that our seventeen-year-old daughter has been posting content online related to Nazi beliefs. She's also in an online relationship with an older, twenty-three-year-old "boyfriend" from Idaho who has influenced her in ways we are just now learning about. We're shocked and very concerned. Kassandra is a good kid, maybe a loner and a little awkward, but she's not hateful. Please help.*
>
> —Jack

His feet planted in his terry cloth morning slippers, hair still damp from a shower twenty minutes before, Jack stepped aside to let his next-door neighbor Mitch through the front door.

"Morning, pal! What's brought you over so early, Mitch? Is the homeowners' association threatening to fine me again because my grass is too long?" Jack joked, not yet aware of the seriousness of his friend's visit. "No? Must be the aroma of Meredith's cinnamon apple biscuits in the oven that's brought you over, then." Jack gestured for Mitch to join him and his wife in the living room for coffee.

Meredith set her magazine down on the ottoman and asked Mitch if she could pour him a cup.

He declined her offer and eased into an armchair. "I'm afraid this is serious. I need to tell you both something."

"All right, Mitch, what is it?" Jack asked, anxiety brimming as he wondered what his neighbor had come by to tell him at seven on a Sunday morning. Jack lowered himself down onto the sofa next to Meredith. "Everything okay at home?"

"It's about Kassandra." Mitch paused to measure his words. "She's involved in some white supremacy nonsense and is spewing horrible, racist things online. Against Jews and Muslims. It's awful, just awful."

Without giving Jack and Meredith time to digest his bombshell about their daughter, Mitch rushed on. "She seems to be some sort of Nazi sympathizer, or worse—a Holocaust denier."

Meredith slid her hand over her husband's tensing fist to keep him from rising. They listened in stunned silence as their concerned neighbor continued to explain their daughter Kassandra's situation in chilling detail. A childhood classmate—a Jewish girl from the same upper-middle-class gated community in Trenton, New Jersey, where the family lived—had stumbled across an anti-Semitic video online and recognized Kassandra's face. After following the link, she discovered a dozen more disturbing videos on Kassandra's YouTube page. Word of her neo-Nazi rantings spread throughout the family's predominately Jewish community and, within hours, an emergency neighborhood meeting convened to discuss the threat Kassandra posed. Mitch slept on it overnight, after which he decided to warn Jack and Meredith about their daughter's activities and the not-so-neighborly pitchforks headed their way.

The revelation shocked Jack and Meredith. Like her identical twin, Simone, Kassandra never exhibited any hateful behavior or said such disturbing things out loud before.

Jack rose from his chair, tugging at his jowls as if teasing loose a knotted rope. "Wait a minute, Mitch. Are you saying one of our girls is a *Nazi?*" He paced around the room behind his neighbor. "This must be a mistake or some cruel practical joke. Someone has lost something in translation. You've known us and our girls since they were born. For Christ's sake—Kassandra? She couldn't be doing what they're accusing her of."

"I saw her saying these things in the videos, Jack. We all did. I'm sorry, but there's no denying it's Kassandra. I saw one where she said Jews are like cancer, and then she faces the camera and salutes Hitler, the maniac who annihilated half my family. Many Jewish families in our community also lost loved ones to Nazi horrors. You can imagine how *meshugana* they all are this morning." Mitch frowned. "Listen, you *are* good people. I know Kassandra is a good kid. I just wanted to let you know before it escalated."

Jack squinted, angry. "What the hell are you talking about?"

"There was talk last night of involving the police, Meredith." Mitch turned to her to plead. "The high school kids are upset. God forbid, I'm afraid of what they might do. You know how impulsive teenagers are."

Jack slumped down into a chair, the momentum nearly toppling him backward. "And now there's an angry mob gunning for our daughter," he murmured, shaking his head in his hands.

"It's some kind of crazy political nonsense she's gotten herself into," Mitch explained. "I don't understand it, but her videos have a bunch of 'Trump for President' campaign stuff mixed in with garbage about dropping immigrants into volcanoes and establishing part of America as a white homeland. You know I'm a Trump guy like you, Jack, but I had to look away—it was too much." Mitch choked up, clearing his throat and drawing a deep breath.

"This is insane!" Jack clamored. "Kassandra doesn't even like politics. She bugs out to her bedroom when we watch the news on television. We're God-fearing Republicans. We hate no one. This is ridic—"

"Thank you for letting us know, Mitch," Meredith cut in, grabbing Jack's hand again. He turned to his wife for support and saw a befuddled gape had settled on her face. "I assure you, we will talk to

Kassandra right away and make sense of this. We're awful sorry for any trouble this caused anyone. Please extend our concerns."

"All right. Let me know if I can help," Mitch said, "besides keeping the angry villagers from breaching your moat." He laughed mechanically before excusing himself.

"Jack," Meredith whispered once Mitch left, her hand finally releasing its grip on his. "I think I saw something strange on Kassandra's computer last week."

Jack's head rebounded as if rear-ended by a semi. "What do you mean you saw something?"

The shock of learning their teenage daughter was a neo-Nazi Internet propagandist was rivaled only by Jack and Meredith's frustration at having missed the warning signs of Kassandra's radicalization. But there weren't many clear indicators to speak of—at least as far as radical ideology was concerned.

What Kassandra's parents, even her identical twin, Simone, had missed was something else in plain view all along. She took her first steps in a long, solitary walk toward extremism *years* before making her hateful videos or meeting her Nazi recruiter boyfriend online. The red flags unfurled early in Kassandra's childhood, but no one noticed.

# 2

## What Leads Us to Extremism

### *Kassandra*

At the time of seventeen-year-old Kassandra's radicalization into white nationalism, her father, Jack, was busy most weekdays selling business software and servers to insurance clients, while overnighting in corporate hotels up and down the Atlantic Seaboard. Her mother, Meredith, a former New York City public school teacher, on the other hand, was home often, having traded in her teaching rubric just five months before the devastating attacks on September 11, 2001, to raise the couple's identical twin newborns.

Kassandra and her sister, Simone, were model children growing up: studious, talented, bright, and well mannered. Like all kids, they came with their share of challenges, too. The twins could disobey the rules, argue about bedtime and belongings, and they sometimes sassed their parents, going from being difficult one minute to charming the next. But they were inseparable growing up and defended each other no matter what the other one did. Kassandra and her sister were the children of a typical—if not privileged—American family.

"I don't know where we went wrong as parents with Kassandra," Meredith later recalled.

As an infant, Kassandra's sister, Simone, tried new things without a fuss. She was thoughtful and quick to giggle with strangers. Kassandra, on the other hand, preferred solitary observation from afar and shared few meaningful relationships other than with her twin. When the girls started kindergarten, Simone made a beeline to play with the toys and see what the commotion was about, while Kassandra retreated to a corner, overwhelmed by the randomness of every new experience. Both girls were excellent students throughout elementary school, but where her sister shone in social circles and sports, Kassandra showed no interest in making friends or taking part in extracurricular activities.

Kassandra kept mostly to the solitude of her bedroom to play her violin, which she did with incredible skill and determination. From an early age, she showed remarkable talent. Jack and Meredith found a private instructor to help develop her gift, and she excelled under the tutelage of an elderly fiddle maestro from the Bronx. Music was Kassandra's way of expressing herself and of latching onto something personal, and she allowed the obsession to consume her. Simone and Meredith shared some of her musical talents, but it was Kassandra who shone in that department. Since it was rare for the twins to get into mischief, Jack and Meredith never worried about Kassandra's growing tendency to spend all her time alone in her bedroom.

But as the girls got older, their social personalities diverged further.

When they entered middle school together, the popular crowd embraced Simone and she made new friends with ease, while Kassandra, because of her intense awkwardness, hated the experience. Even the daily ritual of entering the glass front doors of the private day school she and Simone attended filled her with panic. Classes became more brutal to endure with each passing school day. Over time, Kassandra's ability to hold out until the final bell of the day deteriorated. She craved the safety and seclusion of her bedroom.

To soothe her anxieties while at school, Kassandra sat alone in the cafeteria during lunch period instead of with her sister and their classmates. Lonely and lost inside her head, she fantasized about Simone and her new friends. Studying them, she felt she was smarter and more talented than they were—prettier, too—even if they were more popular. They were fake, reckoned Kassandra. Like a counterfeit Stradivarius violin, the girls at school were nothing more than hollow shells with no souls. Now her twin, Simone, was a fraud, too.

Kassandra's perception—her fantasized reality, that is—was that her female classmates tormented her for years, though Simone swears she witnessed none of the alleged taunting or bullying, and the two girls were rarely apart. "I suppose it could have happened while I was on swim team or involved in dance troupe in fifth and sixth grades," Simone rationalized to her parents. Presenting an interesting dichotomy, Kassandra's pain seemed to stem from the severe *lack* of attention from her classmates, not from any targeted abuse or bullying on their part. Combined with Simone's increasing popularity and blossoming independence, which Kassandra interpreted as the ultimate betrayal, the intense jealousy sliced her deeply. Kassandra never thought—or knew how—to communicate her confusing feelings of alienation, so she had lashed out and projected her frustrations onto others instead.

Near the end of eighth grade, Kassandra began to argue fiercely with her parents to allow her to withdraw from school and complete her remaining classes online at home. She claimed she felt forced to share classrooms with "Barbie dolls" who teased and bullied her. She fought even harder when Jack and Meredith pushed back, trying to convince them she needn't waste any more precious time around the "slutty Jew girls" who bragged about their wild parties and which Shapiro brother they kissed while their parents went away to the Catskills on weekends. Kassandra especially hated *those* girls.

Although she was sure that her female classmates were saying and doing horrible things and plotting to hurt her given a chance, the unsettling truth is, despite how real it felt to Kassandra, none of what she claimed ever happened. Her childhood peers may not have included Kassandra in their activities like they did Simone but they never tormented her. More significant, signaling a clear move toward danger, was the warning sign of Kassandra's new anti-Jewish language. It slipped by her parents and her twin, who brushed it off as typical teenage drama.

Kassandra wore down Jack and Meredith with her tantrums throughout her high school years enough that they eventually relented and allowed her to complete her senior year classes online. But tension continued to build between Kassandra and her parents, and once she turned seventeen, her toxic behavior made a seismic shift.

Experts who study trends in extremism have proposed a multitude of theories about why people hate and how someone without a history of bigotry or intolerance can adopt a hateful ideology and decide to use violence in support of it. Because hate, like most things, is complicated, opinions about how someone becomes radicalized are just as varied and complex.

Harvard University researchers have reported that hateful behaviors form during early childhood and are primarily learned inside the home environment.* I have witnessed this dynamic firsthand in Klan families, where organized hate can be generational—and certainly "casual" racism can be learned from family—but I believe it's a general misnomer that hate is usually "learned at home." I have found, with people I knew in the white-power movement when I was an extremist and with those I've since worked with to disengage from extremism, that hateful extremist behaviors most often take a foothold outside of the purview of one's family. Where this behavior results from youthful rebellion, I find it often manifests as the opposite of what the family unit holds. Hardly anyone rebels by amplifying their parents' core

---

* J. H. Burnett III, "Racism Learned," *Boston Globe,* June 10, 2012, https://www.bostonglobe .com/business/2012/06/09/harvard-researcher-says-children-learn-racism-quickly /gWuN1ZG3M40WihER2kAfdK/story.html.

values. Even when racism stems from the values instilled at home by family, it is still a learned behavior and not an inherent trait of our DNA. No human being comes wired at birth with ideology. No one is "born to hate."

Some researchers have claimed the recent uptick in hate-related incidents can be traced to out-of-control Internet culture.* Others blame toxic masculinity and a strict adherence to male gender roles in generations of young men, which they say stunts the expression of emotion beyond anger.† Disenchanted young, white males finding one another in online "fringe networks" as digital tribesmen fighting a brutal culture war is also a common premise.‡ Experts have also theorized that the absence of positive male role models and the breakdown of "traditional family values" might be key contributors to young men developing aggressive, extremist-like tendencies.§ Some researchers also believe radical ideological or religious views are developed through both personal grievances (either tangible or perceived) and life's general uncertainties,¶ and that environmental factors like poverty, unemployment, or the absence of healthy relationships are all the push one needs to become a violent radical.** There are those who indicate that mental health and psychological disorders might be primary

---

* M. L. Ybarra, M. Diener-West, D. Markow, et al., "Linkages Between Internet and Other Media Violence with Seriously Violent Behavior by Youth," *Pediatrics* 122, no. 5 (2008): 929–937.

† S. Mahmood, "The Link Between Masculinity and Violent Extremism," *Today,* September 10, 2018, https://www.todayonline.com/commentary/link-between-masculinity-and-violent -extremism-0/.

‡ S. Burley, "Wolf Age," *Commune,* August 2019, https://communemag.com/wolf-age/.

§ J. Leving, "Absent Fathers & Youth Violence," *Leving's Divorce Magazine,* March 5, 2009, http://divorcemagazine.wordpress.com/2009/03/05/absent-fathers-youth-violence/.

¶ J. M. Norman, and D. Mikhael, "Youth Radicalization Is On the Rise. Here's What We Know About Why," *Washington Post,* August 28, 2017, https://www.washingtonpost.com /news/monkey-cage/wp/2017/08/25/youth-radicalization-is-on-the-rise-heres-what-we -know-about-why/.

** A. Falk and J. Zweimüller, *Unemployment and Right-Wing Extremist Crime,* IZA Discussion Papers 1540 (Bonn, Germany: IZA, 2005), http://ftp.iza.org/dp1540.pdf.

factors linked to the rise of extremist-related violence and terrorism. Even divisive politics and hyper-partisan rhetoric have been credited for the recent surge in hate-related activities, pointing to the words (or lack thereof) of politicians as the catalyst.

While there is no single profile or surefire predictor that can determine *who* will embrace extremism or develop extremist behaviors, my colleagues are all correct in that they recognize some form or expression of personal trauma as the primary driver of an individual's descent into extremism. Similarly, my theory of *pre-radicalization,* which I have built over three decades working with active and former extremists (myself included), suggests that life's "potholes," caused by unresolved emotional, psychological, and/or physical trauma, and the weighty aftereffects of shame and uncertainty that often accompany trauma, are what push some of us down the road to radicalization. That said, the *trauma journey* toward extremism begins long before any doctrine takes us for a ride.

We all experience these metaphorical potholes. They are the untreated wounds—deep cuts and bruises, singular or cumulative—that are buried deep inside of us; the painful voids and obstructions keeping us from feeling self-worth, security, experiencing greater meaning in our lives, or establishing healthy connections with others. These types of traumatic stressors emerge from emotional and physical abuse, grief, isolation, neglect, loss, challenges with mental health, disability, poverty, even unchecked wealth or privilege, and plain old ignorance, among a variety of other ailments that affect the human condition. These seemingly impassable obstacles can stop us from pursuing positive and life-affirming pathways. Sometimes, if we encounter enough potholes—or even a single, profound one—and we are unable to access the proper resources to repair and navigate around them, they can detour even the smartest, most innocent, or well-meaning down a treacherous road.

At the core of every radicalized individual I have ever met is one commonality: they sought to fill the emptiness caused by traumatic life experiences with *something* to mute or mask their pain. In almost every instance, path-altering potholes were the source of shame or uncertainty that detoured them to where extremist narratives dominated and comforted them—much like an illicit ideological drug might. Often with inadequate outlets to maintain their potholes, they found themselves embraced with open arms by hate movements offering them a sense of safety, camaraderie, and agency—sometimes for the first time in their lives.

For the millions of disillusioned young people today who struggle with peer acceptance or isolation, or who feel relegated to the outermost fringes of society because of personal trauma, social anxiety, bullying, or untreated psychological or emotional disorders, potholes can force an internalization of pain and emotion. Some people end up expressing this hurt through self-harm, drug abuse, crime, or suicide, while others self-medicate by projecting their pain onto others to achieve a similarly numbing effect. Although "extremism" in the more traditional sense comes framed by ideological radicalism or militant religious fundamentalism, other destructive behaviors like abuse (physical, sexual, or emotional), criminality, or addiction can manifest as extremist behaviors in place of, or in addition to, radical ideological beliefs. And like other behaviors we might adopt as pain management for our wounds—bigotry, cults, religious fundamentalism, xenophobia, or the murder of a cafeteria full of students—potholes don't discriminate.

During the stage I call *pre-radicalization,* crashing into life's potholes conditions us to adopt maladaptive or extremist-like behaviors as quick fixes for emotional suffering. Still, trauma in its strictest form isn't solely what diverts a person toward extremism. Potholes *and* an imperiled search for identity, community, and purpose (ICP) are what send us swerving. Though it most often occurs during the uncertainty of youth, when adolescents begin to make their way into the world outside of the home and develop their own ICP, pre-radicalization can happen to any of us at any life stage.

The acquisition of ICP is also important in explaining the typical age range of most extremist or gang recruits, which is twelve to sixteen years old, when one is arguably the most idealistic and impressionable. During this formative life stage, it's also common for young people pre-radicalized by their potholes to take part in a phenomenon I call *cult hopping*, where idealistic but wayward youth—"marginalized seekers"—who are lost in their search for ICP jump from one extremist lifestyle to another. This is common and potentially dangerous for teenagers like young Kassandra, who once revealed to me she considered joining the so-called Islamic State (ISIS) before settling on the neo-Nazi movement—because white supremacy seemed like a "less dusty endeavor."

Although one can understand why Jack and Meredith initially could not believe their daughter Kassandra was a white nationalist, they were grateful for their friend Mitch's warning once the initial shock of it wore off. By letting them know in private about the concerns of their neighbors and trying to stop a vigilante intervention, Mitch gave Jack and Meredith an opportunity to discuss the issue with Kassandra before it turned ugly in that regard. Had the community response been too aggressive, it could have compounded the problem and solidified Kassandra's narrative of victimhood. The warning instead gave her parents time to investigate the claims and address their concerns with Kassandra before any irreversible damage occurred for their daughter, their family, or the community.

Having raised two boys of my own, I can understand how denial might be a parent's typical first reaction when their child's character comes into question. Parents and guardians can misinterpret this as an attack on their parenting skills, or they may have trouble processing the information if it doesn't align with what they already believe is true. It's not that they don't care or aren't concerned about the claim; it just doesn't mesh with their current understanding of the truth. Psychologists call this response *cognitive dissonance,* or the psychological reaction a person experiences when they're faced with a situation where contradictory beliefs or ideas present themselves. This form of mental stress becomes activated when a person accepts new evidence that challenges their current values, while also maintaining old, opposing contradictions as truth. It's common, and we've all experienced this kind of irrational psychological response to varying degrees. Cognitive dissonance is typically only problematic when we don't recognize it when it happens. If we acknowledge it and use it as a learning moment, rather than an opportunity to double down on poor judgment, it can help us better understand ourselves on a deeper level and ferret out assumptions, informing the values and beliefs we hold dear. If we cannot refocus the tension or correct our biases when they occur, we can end up building walls to protect ourselves that we then justify by inventing invaders.

We tend to assume that what we believe about the people closest to us is the unadulterated truth and the only version of acceptable reality is the one we currently hold. I understand why some people find it difficult to accept that their loved ones have become radicalized. It's not pleasant to admit someone you care about is an extremist. We're often too confident—especially as parents—in believing we would notice if something were so wrong with our own kids. Jack and Meredith were no different. Simone struggled with the revelation just as much, stunned by her identical twin's extremist proclivities.

But when Meredith and Jack found Kassandra's YouTube channel, the evidence they saw was indisputable. There was their daughter peddling hate and conspiracy theories to throngs of adoring white nationalists in dozens of videos shot and edited in the privacy of her bedroom—a mere twenty paces from where her parents enjoyed morning coffee. They watched in horror as the young girl they thought they knew unraveled before them.

After watching her videos, Jack and Meredith called Kassandra into the kitchen. Forcing themselves to remain calm, they confronted her about the accusations and told her how they came upon the materials she was distributing. To their heartbreak, Kassandra didn't deny making the anti-Semitic videos. She emphasized instead how proud she was to have made them. Kassandra was confident that if her parents and sister would just hear her out, they'd agree with her theories on "the destruction of white identity" and "the Balkanization of a once-great American homeland." From Kassandra's point of view, her family members were acting foolishly in the face of the genocide of their white race. *They* were the ones who sounded crazy, falling for the lies fed to them by the mainstream media—not her. Didn't they realize a secret cabal of Jews controlled the world? She became incensed at their unwillingness to fight when the stakes were so great. Especially now that they knew the truth.

"Are you out of your mind?" Jack pressed his daughter as Meredith consoled her.

While hate is a subjective emotion, I know Kassandra didn't really hate Jews—she just believed she did. The Jewish girls she grew up going to school with did nothing to feed Kassandra's hatred of Jews. Her anti-Semitism emerged from her feelings of disenfranchisement from the popular girls at school—who coincidentally are Jewish—and made worse by her perception that those same girls drove a wedge between her and her sister, Simone. Kassandra solved her pain equation by concluding that "Jews" were responsible for her trauma, and they became emblematic as the source of her discomfort.

It was not logical for Kassandra to draw such conclusions. Her potholes had developed throughout her entire adolescence, in part because of her loneliness and disconnection, but certainly not because of any harmful actions from her classmates or *any* Jewish people for that matter. Kassandra spent her entire childhood believing she was worthless and strange, and as she and her twin got older and Simone's interests took her in a different direction, naturally growing apart amplified Kassandra's feelings of isolation. This also worsened Kassandra's social anxiety, which broke her down to the point of scapegoating her troubles away. Her deepening potholes left her struggling in a world of deafening silence for years.

When Kassandra rebuked her parents' attempt to temper her beliefs—and when all else (in their eyes) failed—they tried forcing a change in their daughter's behavior. They punished her and took away all means of fulfilling Kassandra's ICP without addressing her unresolved potholes. Everything they tried failed. Oppressive force, or negative pressure of any kind, rarely works when trying to correct bad habits. Family, friends, colleagues, even strangers, driven by either anger or hope, who push an individual to adopt a different set of values, often alienate that person more, shoving them further toward an extreme position. The more cornered Kassandra felt, the fewer options for relief appeared reasonable to her. She entered a self-preservation mode in which she became more entrenched inside the bunker she had sought for safety, where she knew at least some comfort existed. The embattled relationship with her parents became like a tug-of-war contest in quicksand. The more Jack and Meredith pushed and pulled, the quicker Kassandra sank.

Just as disturbing to her grief-stricken parents was their discovery of the source of "truth" Kassandra had accepted. Without their knowledge, she started an online relationship with a college boy from Idaho—a Nazi—named Jakob Bergsson. Jack and Meredith listened with sunken hearts as their daughter told them about her new boyfriend and how he loved her and wanted to make her his wife. It didn't matter to Kassandra that she was still under the legal age of consent and her boyfriend was twenty-three—their six-month digital love affair transcended such trivial nuisances.

Kassandra believed that Jakob, her first ever boyfriend, loved and respected her—unlike her parents and sister, whom she claimed never loved her at all. Though she hadn't met Jakob in person or seen his face over live video during their six months together, she became convinced he knew her better than anyone else did. Soon, they would be together forever, she hoped. Even if it was taking Jakob quite a long time to replace the broken webcam on his computer, his daily emails, occasional snapshots, video messages, and late-night phone calls were enough to keep her pining for his affection.

Kassandra embraced white-supremacist ideology once its community welcomed her in. The promise of acceptance pulled her down an infinite rabbit hole of paradox and contradiction until she could no longer distinguish fantasy from reality, or who it was that loved her and cared about her well-being.

Much like how America's current crisis with violent extremism materialized while we went about our daily routines, Kassandra's potholes and her growing despondency had gone unnoticed and unaddressed since birth. Despite Meredith and Jack being doting parents who provided their children with a wealth of opportunity and nurturing, they missed the internalized chaos of their daughter's life—and the remedies she found to soothe herself. They hadn't thought to shield her from predators inside the presumed safety of their own home. Even if her parents had seen something going wrong with Kassandra—they did at times try to find help for her anxiety during her adolescence—they could not have predicted her downward spiral into white nationalism.

With just one click of a link in the comments section of a Facebook group, Kassandra went from watching videos about teen depression to creating a new user profile on Stormfront—a white-supremacist web forum whose supporters celebrate mass murderers and revel in a coming race war. Once inside, Kassandra adopted a new identity and found what she believed was a welcoming community, and, for the first time, a clear purpose for her life: to save her dying white race from the parasites who were hell-bent on destroying it.

Perhaps more significant to Kassandra, Stormfront was also where she met the man she believed loved her—the Nazi ghost named Jakob Bergsson.

I would soon learn that Bergsson did not just come for Kassandra but for all of us.

# 3

## The Hate We See

### *Daniel*

TURMOIL FILLED YOUNG DANIEL'S EVERY DAY from the moment
he was born. His sister was excited to have a new baby brother in the
house, but he overwhelmed his young mother, Janet. His father, Bud,
who spent most hours at home on the porch drunk, wasn't much help
raising the kids. When Janet sought Bud's support, the alcohol and
ineffective drugs he took to quiet chronic back pain exacerbated his
nastiness toward Janet and the kids.

Daniel's parents argued and emotionally abused each other throughout
his childhood. His father claimed he couldn't work because of a back
injury from a motorcycle accident, while Janet fought like hell for
minimum-wage bar jobs to keep the family above Louisville's poverty
line. It was an uphill battle, considering their part of rural Kentucky
was already one of the most impoverished areas with the highest
unemployment rates in America.

Some of Daniel's potholes growing up were obvious: poverty,
general lack of opportunity, and questionable role models. Others were
deep and had little to no distance between them, like the emotional
abuse he was a constant witness to between his parents. If Daniel was
fortunate enough to evade one pitfall by suppressing his shame, the
likelihood of him stumbling into others, which seemed to multiply by
the day, was almost inevitable.

Finding the same comfort that kept her husband numb, Janet also turned to the bottle and drugs to cope with the overwhelming demands of her life. With parents too intoxicated or disempowered by their struggles with addiction and poverty to attend to their needs, Daniel and his sister were more likely to witness a shouting match at home than experience a family hug. In place of love and stability, years of abuse and aggression had left stains of humiliation and uncertainty. The few books his parents kept in their cramped one-bedroom apartment were used as beer coasters and joint-rolling trays instead of for bedtime stories. Even toys represented a source of fear for Daniel. If his father tripped over one of the few thrift-store finds his son had to play with, Bud would kick whatever it was straight into the wall, leaving a dent in the plaster to remind Daniel not to inconvenience him again.

Daniel's childhood wasn't all misery, though. Love existed and revealed itself at the most unexpected moments. Sometimes, after a few shots of bourbon, Bud might pull Janet in for a kiss. Daniel would pretend to be embarrassed but it tickled him to glimpse genuine affection between his mom and dad. Though it was futile, he hoped it would be the one time their chemical-fueled romance would not turn toxic. But it always did.

Bud never laid a hand on his wife or the children; instead, he emotionally battered them. Janet took on full financial responsibility and kept the family fed by pouring shots and draft beer in biker dives, sometimes pulling multiple shifts in a day. After Bud used up the family's income to attend to his vices—alcohol, cocaine, and the Harley-Davidson chopper he'd been rebuilding for a decade—rent and the cost of feeding four hungry mouths consumed what remained of Janet's small paychecks. It angered Bud, and he blamed her for never having enough money for his pills and booze.

There were after-school programs and aid organizations Daniel's parents could have leveraged for him but didn't. Their corner of Louisville comprised poor black kids and Southern whites like them—poor or otherwise—who had become conditioned, consciously or not, to maintain segregation, so Daniel never attempted to make friends with anyone but the white kids at school. Racial tension simmers close to the surface in the South, so Bud showed his son how to defend himself with his fists and to launch the word *nigger* as a weapon of war.

Before Daniel reached high school, Bud and Janet split up. It was a relief to not live with the constant anxiety of shouting matches between his parents, but the inconsistency of not having his father around made Daniel's potholes worse. Just living was a source of tension, and a stomach full of food often a luxury he couldn't afford, but not having Bud there left Daniel confused and angry about who he was. While Daniel didn't miss the stress of his parents coming to verbal blows, he longed for those few occasions where his mother and father, however imprudent they were, tried to guide him to be better than they had been. Now he hardly saw his dad, and Janet's three jobs meant she was seldom home. When she was there, she was usually drunk and spent time with random men she'd picked up at work.

A year after Janet and Bud split, doctors diagnosed Bud with pancreatic cancer. No matter what he'd done to her, Bud was her children's father, and Janet still cared about him. Even if she also enjoyed romances with other men who hung around the bar till closing, Bud had been the love of her life since high school. So, when he could no longer care for himself, Janet let him live out his last months with her and their children in her tiny Section 8 apartment.

For five months, Daniel watched his father, the only man who'd ever shown concern for him, grow sicker and weaker. It was painful for Daniel, but to his surprise, even though his mother continued dating other men, he also witnessed a kind of intimacy and tenderness between his parents he'd not seen before. At seventeen, Daniel dropped out of school to find work, proud to help support his family. He loved them, no matter how flawed they were. That was normal life for him. "I care about them more than anything," he later told me. "They're all I got."

One morning when Bud wasn't snoring like he usually did, Daniel knew death had claimed his father. He didn't take his passing well. Life had dealt the family yet another brutal blow.

A short time after Bud died, Janet committed herself to starting a new life. Getting clean from drugs and alcohol was the most difficult challenge she would ever face but she knew she had to be strong for her children. Janet's plan also included caring for her new grandson—whose absentee birth father was replaced by an abusive, codependent boyfriend—until her daughter could kick her own drug habit and get back on her feet. Although Daniel never liked his sister's black ex-boyfriend, he loved having a baby nephew around. He tried his best to adapt to this new variation of family.

Daniel remained close with his nephew and sister throughout his teen years, but significant potholes also veered him toward street fighting and old-fashioned bigotry. He cropped his hair short like the rowdy skinheads he spied across the Ohio River in Cincinnati, the ones who drank beer under an overpass where he rode his bike on weekends.

When Janet came home with an old flame a few weeks before she entered detox, Daniel melted down at the sight of the black man with his mother.

The same lover had abused Janet in the past. His attacks were physical, different from how Daniel's father had verbally abused her throughout their marriage. During an earlier affair Janet had with the same man, Daniel witnessed him slap his mother around, shoving her into a door and knocking it from its hinges. After Janet ended their relationship the first time, thirteen-year-old Daniel, perhaps in a bid for his parents' attention, spent the next six months playing what Janet described as a game where he smashed his forehead into the bedroom wall to see how many hits he could take before drawing blood or breaking the plaster. His father had been too drunk to notice or too busy arguing with Janet about the "nigger" he'd caught her with again.

Now, four years after the violent incident, just shy of Daniel's eighteenth birthday, his father was dead and Janet was back with the same abusive boyfriend. Furious at the sight of them together in his mom's parked car, Daniel chose to punish the black man instead of examining himself for the source of his rage. Responding in the only way he'd ever learned, Daniel pounced. Pulling the boyfriend through an open window of Janet's vehicle, Daniel dragged him across the parking lot and beat the man's face with clenched fists until his knuckles bled.

A week later, Daniel went looking for the gang of white-power skinheads from across the river, and he found them. The older members welcomed him like a son. It didn't take long to complete the "tough look" Daniel admired from afar, one that included swastikas and other hate imagery tattooed on his arms, neck, and face.

Though it's likely that Daniel's ideological base was rooted in his father's bigotry—and the pungent stench of racism that still haunts Kentucky and other regions of the former Confederacy—his pre-radicalization trajectory took many sharp turns early in his adolescence. But it was the emotional trauma of seeing his mother belittled by his father, who died before Daniel could process the chaos of their relationship that formed the final pothole that blew out his tire and sent him into a tailspin toward extremism.

The empowerment Daniel experienced through his association with violent skinheads provided him with what he felt was "permission" to express his swirling grievances and the directive to focus his pent-up rage onto a tangible enemy—one he learned to blame for his pain.

The cycle of abuse for Daniel and his family was both generational and environmental. Though I suspect they had hoped to do things differently, the circumstances of their lives had long conditioned them to use atypical means to overcome uncertainty and insecurity. Whatever their reasons, they could not access the proper resources to help them nor did they have the knowledge that help might exist for them. Like so many American families, they felt stuck. And the more they struggled, the deeper into the mire they sank. To control the abuse they themselves endured, they learned to become abusers themselves—abusers of drugs, abusers of one another. And for Daniel, an abuser of self-hatred and shame.

Though it's not fair to equate the plight of Daniel's family to the institutional and systemic racism that still burdens people of color in America today, their situation illustrates how poor whites can also become trapped in cycles of misery and violence by an apathetic system that keeps the impoverished poor and makes the rich richer. The high rates of alcoholism and addiction, patterns of domestic abuse, crime, imprisonment, and social stigmatization stemming from the struggle to attain vital resources, to overcome chronic unemployment, or to just fight for survival are endemic to poverty and independent of race.

Extremists understand these socioeconomic dichotomies exist, and they see vulnerable people like Daniel as easy marks for recruitment to their cause—the low-hanging fruit whose unstable conditions make them prone to accepting (empty) promises of "paradise on Earth" or a return to past greatness. Extremist propagandists exploit the frustrations of people and manipulate them through their endemic uncertainties: lack of meaningful employment, immigration, and the outsourcing they claim threatens those jobs and a family's security, as well as the "elites" they claim have betrayed people into these dismal conditions with lies.

In my work with all sorts of extremists, I have noticed that those who are at risk of losing something are often more susceptible to radicalization than those who don't have discernable means or who feel overwhelmed by the challenges of everyday survival. Similarly, Eric Hoffer—the longshoreman turned influential social philosopher—states in *The True Believer,* his seminal book on mass movements, that people on the cusp of socioeconomic classes are the most vulnerable to recruitment by extremist narratives.* Fear of loss—status, a job, a loved one, freedom, the primary comforts, or privilege—makes individuals living on the edge of society's

---

* Eric Hoffer, *The True Believer: Thoughts on the Nature of Mass Movements,* 1st ed. (New York: Harper and Row, 1951).

spectrum (i.e., the disappearing middle class) easier to seduce. Through the fearmongering tactics of ideologues that paint "others" as disruptive invaders of the status quo, or the hawking of invented memories of past greatness, for some, this is when the fight to maintain their personal certainty trumps fact and logic, and why the once rational suddenly appear mindless.

Renowned social psychologist and my dear friend and mentor, Dr. Arie Kruglanski, describes in his book *Psychology of Terrorism* how Western nations have made grave errors in the fight against terror with their unwillingness to understand that the roots of extremist behavior stem from isolation and grievance and form long before there is any focus on ideology. Vital to any effort in reducing the escalating violent extremist threat is the need to help repair the damaged foundations of individuals, instead of shunning them or disparaging them with opposing viewpoints.*

This is why arguing or punching away hate doesn't work. It often has the negative effect of aggravating maladaptive behaviors in people who already feel isolated and are in survival mode. Since they are protecting what little control they still feel they have, they are willing to do anything to keep it, and conceding an argument or a fight is not one of them. We must tackle extremism like a public health crisis to build human resilience instead of an all-out "war on terror" if we hope to defeat it in the long term.

Repairing the kind of abusive feedback loop experienced by Daniel's family requires ongoing support and extraordinary patience. Professionals such as counselors and cognitive-behavioral therapists can help teach positive life management skills and thought processes over time—but it isn't always easy when someone's ability to access the support they need is out of reach. Often, the more economically challenged or isolated a community is, the more difficult it can be

---

* J. Victoroff and A. W. Kruglanski, eds., *Psychology of Terrorism* (New York: Psychology Press, 2009).

to access necessary resilience-building resources like counselors, job trainers, mental health therapists, life coaches, or an education. For Daniel—and others in a similar situation—it also requires gaining new perspective from his journey to see his mistakes for what they were—learned behaviors—without becoming so overwhelmed by the shame of his decisions that he gives up on repairing his potholes.

Daniel, as he would eventually learn, had encountered potholes so severe that he found it difficult to steady his ground without outside help. A textbook-dysfunctional childhood with low parental expectations and emotional intelligence, as well as divorce, sex, drugs and alcohol, violence, betrayal, and unsettled grief over the death of his parent made Daniel's life a battlefield marred with emotional craters.

With no good options within reach, he took a chance detour to find a way out of his miserable situation. He chose wrong.

At first, Daniel found that becoming a neo-Nazi skinhead masked his emotional pain and fulfilled his need for a "stable" community. It was a place to belong and feel accepted. The strict extremist ideology offered him false solace for his chaotic life, and his new family's routine of street violence filled him with the perception of power—the same kind he'd seen other men around him wield. Daniel felt a semblance of control for the first time.

Following the strategy of white supremacist leaders in the early 1990s to mainstream their malignant cause, Daniel's more visible brand of white-supremacist extremism is no longer the norm in America. Today's modern era of hate has instead largely camouflaged itself and moved underground.

When I became a neo-Nazi skinhead over three decades ago, nothing filled me with more confidence and pride than the uniform I wore: a shaved head, steel-toed Dr. Martens boots with white straight laces, a black nylon bomber jacket loaded with patches and provocative imagery that left little of what I believed to the imagination, and tattoos.

Lots of them—swastikas, Celtic crosses, and Viking runes—inked into my skin. Like Daniel, I wore pride on my sleeves, figuratively *and* literally.

The generation of militant white supremacists I fought alongside in the 1980s and '90s—including the Klan with their distinctive white hoods, and skinheads—was difficult to miss coming from a mile away. That was by design: our thuggish personas were carefully cultivated, our bouts of violence sparking at the slightest stimulus to strike fear in the hearts of our enemies. Intimidation wasn't just the means to an end—for some, it *was* the end. Yet for every skinhead who only knew how to express emotion through violence, there were scores more who had never been in so much as a shoving match. It hardly mattered; so long as people saw our intimidating exteriors, they remained afraid.

Around the late 1990s, movement leaders began to recognize that high visibility wasn't doing them any favors. Aside from the unwanted attention they began drawing from law enforcement, most white racists—even the covert ones who would behave politely in public but drop the "N-bomb" among friends—considered our intimidating looks and destructive activities too extreme—so extreme we began alienating prospective recruits.

Most of the various factions within the white-supremacist ecosystem recognized this challenge and pivoted. Soon, messaging softened when discussing the "enemies of the people." The tradition of wearing a uniform-like attire for intimidation fell out of favor and was replaced by wardrobes that allowed them to blend in.

Old racist canards about "global Jewish control" became buffed and polished to sound more like conservative foreign policies. Terms like *globalist* and *global elite* replaced *Zionist* and *Jew*. Cries of "White power!" became whispers of white pride. Blatant Holocaust deniers resurfaced as revisionist historians, labeling themselves "skeptics" to influence underground "race realist" movements hiding in pseudo-academic circles on college campuses. Calls to "save the white race" gave way to the deceptive oath of "We the People." Efforts sought to legitimize white supremacy as a form of racial pride, emphasizing the notion of reverse racism—the discredited hypothesis that claims historically privileged groups (whites) are frequently made the targets of racism by policies accounting for racial disparities. Co-opting the civil rights message of Black Lives Matter, the slogan "White Lives Matter" gained favor among white supremacists over the more traditional chant of "*Sieg heil.*" Debunked racist junk science from Charles A. Murray's *The Bell Curve* crawled back from the dead and found new allies in philosophical snake-oil pushers. Misogyny found champions in bestselling "men's rights" authors and anti–political correctness podcasters. Through carefully crafted optics and slick messaging, toned-down "alt-lite" bloggers used race-baiting identity politics to attract millions of unsuspecting new supporters, coaxing them further down the pathway to full-on extremism. Tempered racist propaganda hid behind patriotism, flawed data gave people a supposedly objective weapon to brandish, and uninformed cynicism made stumbling toward increasingly toxic narratives come fast and furious for those wrought with the uncertainty of modern times.

By the latter half of the 1990s, large-scale Klan rallies became scarce and the flamethrower of propaganda that was the white-power music scene of the mid-'90s cooled to an ashy ember. Even reliable white-supremacy watchdog groups like the Anti-Defamation League and Southern Poverty Law Center touted research showing membership of hate groups was on a steady decline. The paradox of skinheads disappearing from alleyways and punk-rock clubs had lulled Americans into a false sense of security.

The metastasis from overt white power to "identity politics" took time. But crafting a less recognizable poison for the disillusioned white masses to swallow became easier when Barack Obama became America's first black president. That's when paranoia among some whites exploded—making them easier to recruit.

During President Obama's first term in office in 2008, a new version of the white-supremacist movement of my youth—a variety that emphasized pride and left the hateful undergirding more implicit—*white nationalism*—began to rear its ugly head.

Mainstream whites living on the more conservative edge of the political spectrum, including Libertarian free speech and small-government aficionados, found the bitterness of white supremacy more palatable in its new form. Anonymous supporters—often college-educated, privileged, young white males (and an increasing number of women, too) started becoming exposed to alt-right ideas through Internet memes on mainstream social media networks like Twitter, YouTube, and Facebook, and online fringe networks like 4chan (and the now defunct 8chan), Reddit, and Gab, where sympathizers revel in political incorrectness and the denigration of multiculturalism, feminism, and immigration, converging on the notion that white identity and the preservation of white racial homogeneity is of sacred importance. Hiding in plain sight, this new hate movement built itself on the same foundation and long-standing principles of old-fashioned American white supremacy.

I often need to remind myself that it's easier for me to see it as a wolf in sheep's clothing because I once played the same disingenuous semantic games when I was a white supremacist. Like many of the movement leaders I worked with back then, who also used terms like *white pride* and *white civil rights* to suggest that pride, not hate, was the movement's driving force, today's leaders are also whitewashing their true intentions. Feigning innocence, people like Richard Spencer—the brash, well-dressed, self-proclaimed leader of the hate movement known as the alt-right—peddle more sanitized extremist messages while arguing they don't hate anyone. They claim to stand for the rights of marginalized whites—like they say other races freely do—to sway vulnerable, wayward youth into becoming new recruits for their cause.

Like today's white nationalists—who sometimes refer to themselves euphemistically as "patriots" or "nationalists"—leaders like myself who set the stage for this transformation encouraged people to disassociate from known hate groups like the KKK, neo-Nazi skinheads, and the various other visible factions, so they could later crawl out from beneath the shadows, dust themselves off, and enjoy the benefits of what they see as something of a duty—a "humanitarian" cause—albeit an incredibly hateful and damaging one.

Many within the white-supremacist ranks joined the US Armed Forces and deployed to Iraq for the first Gulf War, where they gained combat skills and weapons training and recruited fellow soldiers who'd been steered to the enlistment office by their own potholes and precarious quests for ICP. Others were encouraged to enroll in community college or attend universities where they could recruit freshmen eager to form new opinions. Some faded into America and became teachers or lobbyists, intent on corrupting the system from within. They also pursued jobs in law enforcement and the justice system to shield their comrades, should any run afoul of the law. Today, groups like the Three Percenters and the Oath Keepers, far-right anti-government militias claiming membership of thirty-five thousand, comprise first responders, law enforcement, and military personnel—both former and active-duty. More charismatic leaders with clean criminal records ran for political office—and in some cases were successful.

Maintaining the more visible remnants of the white-supremacist movement from my youth, such as the boots-on-the-ground posture Daniel adopted, remained useful for intimidation and branding—or for attracting those drawn to the violence. But its value faded as virtual spaces like social media and multiplayer video games replaced physical recruiting grounds like playgrounds, concert halls, skate parks, and video arcades.

Since then, the strategy to fold a more sanitized white-supremacist narrative into the American mainstream—which took decades to cultivate and continued long after I disengaged—has taken root.

It wasn't an easy sell at first to a bunch of heavily tattooed skinheads and backwoods Klansmen. Some didn't budge and continued the same path; many later ended up dead, in prison, or as dodgy, racist granddads living in one of America's many forgotten trailer parks. Others slid sideways into equally destructive lifestyles—like addiction, crime, or outlaw biker culture.

Skinhead groups like the Hammerskins that Daniel joined (and I once helped lead) are some of the last remaining holdouts from the movement's transition from Doc Martens boots to bespoke suits, and even most of these individuals have now gone underground.

While I know that some of the old-guard white supremacists from my era grew up, found their way out, and ultimately chose to walk a better path—and I'm proud of them for doing so—I also know most did not. We are only now beginning to discover the recesses where these thousands of others disappeared to. I still remember many of the faces I once knew, which sometimes come to me in my thoughts when I least expect them—a familiar smirk over my shoulder in the dusty reflection of a shop window or on the surface of a puddle, rippling from the wind, and then they disappear—and I wonder what violence they might still unleash.

# 4

---

## Hate Becomes Normalized

### *Ben*

WHILE IT'S STILL DIFFICULT TO pinpoint exactly which early potholes may have led to Ben's eventual radicalization, later factors that undeniably contributed included his time spent in prison and the fighting he did on the military battlefield.

A US Army veteran with two tours of duty in Iraq, Ben lost his two closest friends in combat. Compounding those horrific mementos of war was debilitating post-traumatic stress disorder (PTSD). While adolescent potholes may not have diverted Ben toward extremism, his time in combat was rife with setback and loss. Because of the violence and death that he witnessed, war became Ben's most devastating pothole. But it wasn't until after his second deployment ended, when he served time for armed robbery, that an extremist narrative found him.

Ben's best friend died in his arms during his first tour in Iraq after their transport truck hit an improvised roadside bomb set by Ba'ath Party loyalists. Then, six weeks later, another close friend was killed by enemy gunfire in Mosul. The unbearable aftereffects of losing his fellow soldiers—his closest companions—in an exceptional environment of mutual preservation weighed heavily on Ben. He suffered intense survivor's guilt, believing that as their unit leader he should have prevented their deaths. After they died, Ben came to see the war he was fighting in as futile, which magnified his resentment of the government that had put his fellow soldiers in harm's way.

Cocktails consisting of Jack Daniel's and Percocet helped Ben slay the demons in his nightmares after his first tour ended. He'd gone back home to the family horse farm in Yuma, Arizona, hoping to get rid of them altogether. The constant heartbreak over losing his pals, and the spontaneous mental paralysis occurring more frequently now that he was home, only intensified the addictions he developed to mute the horrors he suffered in war. But even the painkillers and whiskey weren't enough anymore to mask the hopelessness he felt. Anxiety immobilized Ben. He missed the action of the battlefield—and his brothers.

Ben felt unsafe being back home in Yuma. His hometown seemed alive with danger—rooftops hid snipers, tranquil roads suddenly dissolved into flashbacks of gunfire and flying shrapnel. That was enough for him to stop driving his pickup truck and start taking taxis when he needed time away from the ranch, which had fallen into disrepair since he enlisted. The horses were gone, sold off for pennies on the dollar to pay back taxes on the property. Now, danger lurked in the empty stables and on the side of the road in debris that could be hiding explosives. The new faces that surrounded him in his dusty town reminded him of those in the desert—of the people he'd learned to distrust. Everything that was once familiar to Ben now signaled jeopardy.

It was difficult for Ben's mother to reconcile the idealistic young man who had enlisted to defend his country with the angry, short-tempered soldier who returned from war jaded and bitter. She treated her son with kid gloves, like he could break at any moment, and was almost formal in her interactions with him like a language barrier existed. Nothing she did put him at ease, and Ben slipped further away. The relationships that once brought him so much joy were replaced by strained interactions too difficult to sustain.

Foreign desert sands and gunfire claimed the once-helpful high school valedictorian as a casualty, and a soured nihilist had emerged in his place. War made conflict easy to define for Ben, but what his life should be like without the sounds and smell of death remained a mystery.

The battlefield played a very important and precise role for Ben—he led his fellow soldiers and was responsible for their safety. Now he felt nonessential, lost and purposeless, when he wasn't blacked-out drunk. The ambiguities of every day felt more dangerous to Ben than combat ever had. So, like too many soldiers who return from war to find civilian life difficult, Ben ran toward relief by placing himself back in the same chaos that had birthed his original trauma—he reenlisted for a second tour.

Ben felt he had failed his brothers on his first deployment. He promised himself he wouldn't let it happen again.

When Ben's second deployment to Iraq ended in early 2007, he again returned to the empty family hacienda in rural Arizona. This time, both the wide-eyed eighteen-year-old and the angry soldier were gone. In their place stood a twenty-three-year-old veteran incapacitated by the psychological shrapnel of war.

A month into his second homecoming and shortly before the anniversaries of his two comrades' deaths, Ben stumbled home again from Dicky's Pub and Pump, like he had every night since coming back. The usual amounts of whiskey and pills hadn't quite hushed the pain, so he rinsed out a mason jar and pulled a bottle of Jack from his cupboard to pour himself another. And a few more. He gulped down a handful of pills—some yellow, some blue—and then some dark red ones, like the color of dried blood, he thought.

"Bottom's up," he grumbled.

Ben stood in his stark kitchen alone, feeling hollow, like he knew less about who he was now than before he'd enlisted the first time. He'd been a scared rabbit back then, just a kid. Things were simpler. Now life meant a fistful of pharmaceuticals washed down by rotgut, and a day didn't pass where he didn't feel terrified.

He pulled the dog tags from around his neck and dropped them into the empty jar. Reaching down for his duffel, he pulled out the black kaffiyeh that had shielded his face from the stinging Anbar Province sandstorms and wrapped it around his neck. He felt around through the jumble of dirty clothes for his loaded .45, the one his late stepdad left him when he passed. Finding the heavy piece of steel wrapped inside a sweatshirt, he buried the gun into his waistband. Ben felt guilty for not having been there to console his mom when she needed help with Pop's funeral arrangements. Even if his parents called him a hero, Ben felt like he had failed everyone—including himself. Something had to give. His head felt heavy.

Ben leaned against the doorframe to catch himself before heading outside to smoke a cigarette and clear his mental fog.

Except for the amber glow of Mexicali lighting up the distant horizon, the streets of Yuma were desolate at 3:45 in the morning. The dense December air hung motionless and cold but unusually humid for Arizona—and far too quiet for Ben.

*That's when the enemy strikes—when you least expect them,* Ben thought, sucking in a lungful of hot tobacco smoke.

The nighttime vehicle checkpoints outside of Mosul breathed the same still, dead air just before the roar of an engine and the high beams of a suicide bomber pierced the dust cloud. He recalled the tearing sound the air made as bullets whipped past his ears. A sharp recollection of the tense posturing Ben felt during his nighttime patrols brought a spasm to his lower spine, putting him right back in the thick of battle—sweat stinging his eyes, the weight of his loaded tactical vest, a weapon gripped in his balled fist. Alert, with a nervous finger alongside his trigger, Ben waited for signs of life—or incoming death—not knowing which one he would find first or what either looked like.

Ben's body trembled in the crisp, foggy Yuma air. His forgotten cigarette, lit and dangling from between his fingers, dropped to the ground as the yellow, four-door sedan crept closer. It stopped and jerked forward, filling the night sky with a foreboding glow, and moving in his direction.

*One hundred meters from the first concertina line,* Ben calculated.

"Lance Corporal Garza, report any BOLOs—over," he said out loud to no one.

*Overwatch should have radioed any outside movement by now.*

But they hadn't. The familiar crackle of radio static was absent.

As the dark-skinned taxi driver stopped his cab at the intersection alongside where he stood, Ben was no longer home in Yuma. In fact, he never really came back.

Heart pounding, Ben wrapped the scarf up around his face. Pistol in hand, he raised it and pointed, approaching the vehicle's open window. When the driver begged for his life in perfect English instead of Arabic, it stunned Ben back to reality. In a flurry, he panicked and shoved the muzzle of the gun into the frightened man's tearful cheek, robbing his palms of the few dollars he'd already offered.

Minutes later, Yuma police arrested Ben without incident as he sat sobbing on a curb less than fifty yards from the crime scene, ashamed of what he did, fearful of the monster he had become.

In court the next morning, Ben didn't bother trying to dodge the judge with excuses. He pleaded guilty to felony armed robbery. Hanging his head, he absorbed the stillness of the courtroom. *Is this what peace feels like?* he wondered.

The judge eventually sentenced Ben to six years in prison. Citing why she hadn't levied the maximum ten-year penalty in her decision, she said that Ben's brave service for America and all he'd left out on the battlefield had already cost him plenty. The court order mandated that a prison psychotherapist treat Ben—if only the lockup they shipped him to had one. Over the thirty-two months that Ben served out his time with good behavior, a volunteer social worker was available to see him only once.

So, he found other ways to work out his problems.

\*   \*   \*

Like the military, Ben found some relief from his demons in the regimented routines of prison life. Both his cellblock and the Army provided three hot meals and equally shitty cots to sleep on, and life in both places came with the risk of death. Though, neither the front line nor prison would silence his demons completely.

Inside the private-run prison complex in nowhere Arizona, dominated by Latino inmates, pale and dead-eyed Ben didn't go unnoticed for long. But it was the small crew of white prisoners, the ones he sat near at chow time out of self-preservation, who sized him up first. Like in most other prison environments, whites stuck with whites because they were outnumbered.

Ben got his first book about white identity from a fellow inmate—an old-school skinhead doing twenty to life for beating a homeless black man into a coma. During the long, hot days stewing in his cell, amplifying his uncertainty, Ben tore through the book *My Awakening* by ex-KKK leader David Duke. Additional writings from Duke and other "race realists"—a more palatable moniker used by pseudo-academic white supremacists to mask their ugly racist intentions—soon followed. The words he read caused a personal awakening in Ben.

Duke's tome exalted white Europeans as the most superior civilization humankind had ever seen and put forth long-debunked IQ junk science as truth. The conspiracy theories that Ben devoured left him believing white people were losing space because of a multicultural Jewish agenda created to destroy them. The propaganda painted white culture with broad strokes of glory and equivocated "white might" as a God-given right. "Facts" from the likes of David Duke spelled out impending doom for "white nations" if they couldn't cull the diseased "mud races" from infecting their herds. Ben came to believe the disease would spread and was being facilitated by the saboteurs of white civilization—namely, Jews, globalists, blacks, and a new breed of "race traitor" that white nationalists like Duke call "social justice warriors," who welcomed their own slaughter with their arms wide open. These traitorous whites, Ben came to believe, licked the boot heels of their Jewish masters and were the tools of "white genocide"—an inflammatory and absurd notion that suggests the disappearance of "whiteness" through mixed-race families, high nonwhite birthrates, and mass migration will amount to a complete decimation of white culture.

The behaviors Ben learned as an effective soldier betrayed him. He found the racist teachings to have the familiar ring of military training, where he swore to protect something and learned to kill all "enemies" who threatened that which he'd sworn to protect. David Duke and the white-power movement also made a clear break between friend and foe. The emotional connections Ben made with other "racialists," both in prison and after his release, were a lot like what he'd felt in war— camaraderie until death for a "great cause" and an "us" against "them" mentality. But, unlike the army, it wasn't a positive community that Ben found in this new brotherhood—it was a type of trauma bonding collective, where misery loves company.

Ben's reading of racist texts, based in the same racist tropes and conspiracies used to indoctrinate me decades earlier, spurred a personal catharsis that rationalized the fierce battle raging inside of him. For months back home in Arizona, Ben felt he was in a war zone. Now, after reading Duke's theories on race, he suddenly understood why. He *was* on a battlefield, he thought, one he hadn't recognized at first. And, now, he was weaponless. Acting like a powerful intoxicant, this revelation reignited Ben's survival instinct and sent him sprinting toward extremism—where he replaced one bloody war with another.

It's no coincidence that eagle-eyed white supremacist recruiters spotted an idealistic and vulnerable young man like Ben. The close-quarters camaraderie and tension/fear of military life and death are comparable to the brotherhood and "race war" narratives offered by white supremacists. In fact, military experience and combat skills are so valuable to extremist movements that savvy recruiters have in some cases shown up to personally welcome home soldiers returning from war, offering them jobs and instant ICP upon arrival.

Extremist movements also appreciate a former soldier's weapons training, their unwavering dedication to a cause greater than themselves, enemy/ally dynamics, and fierce warrior-like attitudes, which they view as critical components needed to defeat the enemy. They offer veterans leadership roles, knowing in some ways that no one is better qualified to train others for a racial holy war at home than those who have been left behind after surviving similar battles on foreign soil. As reported in a study released by the FBI in 2008, white-supremacist leaders have recruited soldiers and recent combat veterans of the wars in Iraq and Afghanistan.* An earlier FBI report from 2006 also flagged the infiltration of law enforcement, further exposing the white-supremacist strategy of blending into first-responder communities.†

Many serving in the military have awoken to the risk of radicalization, seeing their comrades crawling down the path toward ideological extremism. A confidential online survey of over one thousand active-duty troops conducted in 2017 by *Military Times* concluded a month after a white supremacist sped his vehicle through a crowd of anti-racist protesters at the Unite the Right rally in Charlottesville that 42 percent of enlisted respondents ranked homegrown white nationalism as a more pressing national security matter than the wars in Syria, Iraq, or Afghanistan.‡

As America's soldiers like Ben became targets of recruitment, white supremacy also shape-shifted into another dangerous new form. Long before Ben read the words that inspired him to pledge himself to white

---

* *White Supremacist Recruitment of Military Since 9/11* (Washington, DC: Federal Bureau of Investigation, 2008).

† *White Supremacist Infiltration of Law Enforcement* (Washington, DC: Federal Bureau of Investigation, 2006).

‡ L. Shane III, "One in Four Troops Sees White Nationalism in the Ranks," *Military Times*, October 23, 2017, accessed July 1, 2019, https://www.militarytimes.com/news/pentagon -congress/2017/10/23/military-times-poll-one-in-four-troops-sees-white-nationalism -in-the-ranks/.

nationalism, a new era of undercover white nationalism had been set into motion. And it was Ben's ideological mentor and former Klansman David Duke who gave it the nudge.

Arguably the clearest example of modern white supremacy injecting itself into the American bloodstream is the case of David Duke, the former grand wizard of the Louisiana Knights of the Ku Klux Klan. In 1988, Duke shed his traditional Klan wardrobe to don the three-piece suit of a DC politician.

Campaigning on a white-separatist platform, Duke ran as a Republican candidate in a special election in 1989 and won a seat in the Louisiana House of Representatives, where he served for three years. Duke attempted to unseat incumbent J. Bennett Johnston in the 1990 US Senate race and lost, but still received over 40 percent of the vote—and about 60 percent of the white vote.* Duke ran again in 1991, this time eyeing Louisiana's governorship. He finished second in the state's open primary in October of the same year with a sizable 32 percent of votes, landing him in the gubernatorial runoff a month later with three-time former governor Edwin W. Edwards. Although Duke ultimately lost the election, he again won most of the white votes in the state, and seventy-five thousand more overall than he'd received in his US Senate bid the previous year.†

In 2016, Duke announced another run for the Republican nomination for Louisiana State Senate. Claiming he was running to defend the rights of "European" Americans—a scrubbed version of his

---

* J. C. Kuzenski, C. S. Bullock, and R. K. Gaddie, *David Duke and the Politics of Race in the South* (Nashville, TN: Vanderbilt University Press, 1995).

† P. West, "The Numbers from Louisiana Add Up Chillingly Duke's Claim on White Vote Shows Depth of Discontent," *Baltimore Sun*, November 18, 1991, https://www.baltimoresun.com/news/bs-xpm-1991-11-18-1991322072-story.html.

previous proclamation to defend "white" Americans—Duke stated, "I'm overjoyed to see Donald Trump and most Americans embrace most of the issues I've championed for years."

David Duke and his extremist cohort were effective in furthering their undercover racist agenda. By stripping away the hackneyed varnish of their old-fashioned white supremacy and disguising it in more conservative rhetoric, hopeful Americans—either reveling in incremental social progress or sidelined by it—failed to notice they were being hoodwinked.

The decline in hate groups and hate crimes from the mid-1990s until the 2008 election of Barack Obama as president was not the result of progress in race relations, nor was it because of anyone's effectiveness in combating hate. It was instead an orchestrated maneuver by white supremacists to become invisible and infiltrate traditional American life—and it worked.

Upon his release from prison, Ben found like-minded people on the Internet. Through white-supremacist websites like Stormfront and the Daily Stormer, Ben put his skills to work. Despite a heavy influence by the repugnant hate content pumped out by the Daily Stormer and its founding hatemonger, Andrew Anglin—a pale, thirtysomething who revels in the racist underbelly of America—Ben chose to join a less overt "white identity" group. It was not a blatant neo-Nazi crew that met Daily Stormer standards but instead a suit-and-tie college campus club called the European Heritage Front (EHF). Dressing down his wolfish ideas in a subtler outfit, he modeled himself after his idol David Duke.

Ben first made the news in April 2017, when fifty demonstrators— from Donald Trump supporters dressed in LOCK HER UP! T-shirts to flak-jacketed militiamen and swastika-flag-waving neo-Nazis—gathered in Martin Luther King Jr. Park, in downtown Denver, for a "Patriot's

Parade" flash mob sanctioned by EHF. Publicized as a pro-Trump free speech rally, the event drew several hundred counterprotesters, including a large contingent of black-clad, masked anti-fascist—*Antifa*—activists. Police secured the perimeter of the park, but by noon a full-on riot broke out and had spilled into adjacent streets.

Ben, then thirty-one, jumped headfirst into the fray.

A young black pastor, wearing a red bandanna around his face and a white robe stained with grass at the knee where he'd rested it to pray, appeared in front of Ben. Surprised by the man who'd emerged from behind the curtain of tear gas, Ben stepped in, fists clenched, and drew back his arm. His first blow landed squarely on the bridge of the pastor's nose.

The man crumpled to the ground as Ben continued to unload punches on him. A news team that was standing by livestreamed the attack from their website and the clip went viral on social media. It showed a masked Ben in his chestnut-blond buzz cut, clad in black military fatigues and a white-pride T-shirt, as his tattooed arms pummeled an unarmed man of faith.

Scrums of opposing bodies grappled and thrashed around them. Crude shields and improvised weapons cut through the swirling haze, the tangled mass shoving one another to control a square foot of personal ego—or protect it from one. Wooden staffs holding SMASH COMMUNISM protest signs became clubs that pounded nonwhite skin and bones. Peace activists turned road debris into retaliatory projectiles of war. Even though police could have identified Ben in the video, they did not arrest or charge him with any criminal violations. No disorderly conduct or mob action charges were filed, not even a fine levied for disturbing the peace. The viral video of the brawl gave Ben his fifteen minutes of fame, though, and he used every second of it to his advantage.

Ben quickly ramped up efforts to cement his group's power move into the conservative political mainstream. To help "Unite the Right," he would join EHF members in their march at the upcoming alt-right rally in Charlottesville, Virginia. For the first time in Ben's life, the White House seemed to agree with disaffected white Americans. It was his moment. Now, the entire world would see that, despite their attempts to destroy his culture, no matter how hard they tried, they would never replace the white man.

# 5

## White Pride Worldwide

### *Kassandra*

Kassandra placed her violin gently into its velvet-lined case and snapped shut the clasps on its lid. Leaving it secure in the center of her canopy bed, she locked her bedroom door and sank low into her armchair. Her mom and dad seldom questioned the locked door. If Kassandra wanted to do her schoolwork and study in private in her room or practice her music lessons with no interruptions, that was fine with them. She'd preferred solitude since she was a child, and Meredith and Jack learned to adjust to it, as did her twin, Simone.

Resting her fingers on the backlit keyboard, Kassandra logged on to her laptop. After another glance to check the locked door, she opened her web browser, took a long breath, and typed in *www.stormfront.org*. She had stumbled onto the website six months earlier through a link in a depression and mental health discussion group on Facebook she frequented. The headline of the posting read, "Psychology is Jewish," which struck Kassandra as something connected to her struggle with the Jewish girls at school.

Even before Kassandra first landed on Stormfront, she found consolation and camaraderie in the online threads in public web forums like Reddit and 4chan, where users came together to post "humorous" and "ironic" memes that mocked Jews and the Holocaust. She had never thought to question the anti-Semitic and hateful posts the other users made. In fact, they rarely went challenged by forum moderators—and if someone did push back, other forum members trolled them so hard for it, they would often shut down their accounts and disappear forever. Kassandra observed some of this brutal trolling, and she read somewhere in the wasteland of meme culture that for some it was so awful that they changed their names and moved to another country or killed themselves. Kassandra would make sure to comply so the same wouldn't happen to her. She was one of them now and would never betray their trust.

Through a psychological manipulation tactic that counter-extremism and cybersecurity analysts call *memetic warfare,** Kassandra eventually became desensitized by the never-ending barrage of offensive digital propaganda and misinformation she ingested for hours and days on end. The tactic was so effective that as Kassandra was exposed to more overt racism and saw hard-core Nazi propaganda, it hardly fazed her. The language seemed crude and in poor taste to her at first, but the more she immersed herself in the ultra-offensive story lines, the more she ignored her discomfort and accepted the narratives as truth. What happened to Kassandra may also explain why unconscious bias exists in so many otherwise well-intentioned white Americans today—we've learned for so long to ignore the uncomfortable truth about our complicity to racism that we can no longer see how we've assimilated into the white-supremacist power structures we abhor.

The racist websites and forums Kassandra frequented—specifically Stormfront, which is the oldest and largest white-supremacist website on the Internet—are mostly anonymous communities of males who assemble en masse to demonize those they consider different. Users regularly condemn Jews, blacks, gays, Muslims, and liberals, among other minority communities, as the purveyors of all society's ills. The more

---

* D. Olsen, "How Memes are Being Weaponized for Political Propaganda," *Salon,* February 24, 2018, https://www.salon.com/2018/02/24/how-memes-are-being-weaponized-for-political-propaganda/.

Kassandra read the racist epithets, saw "Holo-Hoax" postings claiming the Holocaust was a lie, watched white-identity propaganda videos, and listened to "anti-globalist" conspiracy theory podcasts—digital content that now bombarded her social media feeds like German Stuka pilots—the less the racist vitriol shocked her. Eventually, these Internet hangouts became the places she felt most welcome. As she engaged with other members, she felt seen, respected, even valued—things Kassandra had not experienced in the real world because of lifelong social anxiety. Every time Stormfront lit up her computer screen, Kassandra felt liberated. In those isolated online spaces, she finally felt like she was somebody, and it made her happy, even if it was at the expense of six million slaughtered Jews and the angry liberals who found her new views repulsive.

It was also on Stormfront where Kassandra's radicalization journey took another sharp turn that nearly sent her careening off a cliff. It was where she met Jakob Bergsson.

Kassandra was already brainwashed by her Aryan Prince Charming for six months before I found the opportunity to meet her and her parents in person. During that time, Bergsson had sent her racist poetry and books on the "coming race war," and he learned every detail about her personal life—a privilege no one else shared. She held no secrets from her new boyfriend. As bright as Kassandra was, she believed she learned so much more from Jakob than she ever had from any textbooks or from her parents or sister. Kassandra was excited to pass this new knowledge along to others, which brought the two online lovers closer together. It was Bergsson's idea for Kassandra to make "propaganda" videos, as he called them. She even adored the way Jakob said the word, claiming it sounded "old-timey and sophisticated in his adorable German accent."

In their frequent online chats, Jakob Bergsson "enlightened" Kassandra about the calamitous extinction their white race faced. She used that misinformation and spoke passionately in her videos about her boyfriend's message: Jews, blacks, immigrants, gays, Muslims, and other "mud people" were threatening the existence of her race.

If "woke whites" did not eradicate these "societal diseases" from the planet, as Jakob explained, it would result in the demise of the greatest civilization in history—the white lifeblood of Mother Europe. Jakob believed the only way to halt this genocide was to win back the hearts and minds of the "liberalized white zombie hordes" who were slumbering through their own demise and wetting their pants over a Hillary Clinton presidency. If it was important to Jakob, it became important to Kassandra.

She knew Jakob was proud of her and the small media enterprise he helped her create. Kassandra memorized every passage from the websites he sent her to. The tenets of National Socialism—Nazism—that she absorbed poured out on paper as a script. With Jakob's encouragement, the words spilled from her mouth with rigor and bile. As "Valkyrie Vixen" (Kassandra's online identity), and with Jakob's help, she built up a loyal and feisty following that grew by the day.

I put a plan in motion to identify Jakob Bergsson after speaking with Jack and Meredith about their daughter. They suspended all nonessential Internet access to prevent Kassandra from posting any more videos or engaging with Bergsson. The old Valkyrie Vixen clips stayed up, since forcing Kassandra to take them down meant she would have to log back in with her password and risk the chance of seeing any new messages that might lead her back into his clutches. Through Bergsson, however, her followers had already caught wind she was in trouble with her parents, and they re-uploaded her videos to backup sites in case the originals were removed. Limiting Kassandra's access was a logical first step, but I knew it wasn't a permanent solution. Her bond with Bergsson and his white-supremacist cause involved strong emotions. Keeping Kassandra away from the Internet alone wouldn't be enough of a deterrent to stop her from falling deeper into the movement. Blinded by what she thought was love, we would need more support to extricate her.

As I researched the person who had seduced Kassandra over the Internet, I uncovered an insight I thought would be sharp enough to pierce Kassandra's armor—Jakob Bergsson wasn't real. Whoever she communicated intimately with for six months was a real person, to be sure, but they were disguising their identity. I searched to the point of exhaustion and couldn't find anyone with Jakob Bergsson's name anywhere who matched any of the characteristics he communicated in his social media profiles. Whoever Bergsson was, the alias he was using was fake and he was not in love with Kassandra; he was exploiting her. If I could prove to her that she was communicating with a troll who was using the Jakob Bergsson persona to fool her into doing his bidding, I thought, perhaps it would be enough to wake her up. She had been recruited and groomed specifically to be a pitch person for pro-white propaganda. Far from a boyfriend, the entity called Jakob Bergsson was her handler. His job was to find and lure pretty, young girls into becoming propaganda mouthpieces, the end goal being to recruit more young males through the videos the girls made.

Naïve and desperate for connection, Kassandra fell for the scam. To tell her what I'd learned without solid proof of Jakob Bergsson's real identity might drive her deeper underground and push her away from the positive outlets she needed.

With Jack and Meredith's permission, I started communicating with Kassandra over video chat before arranging to meet them in person. I let her know that I understood her situation and explained her parents had asked me to help them navigate the world she entered. While digging for information on Bergsson, I continued to establish a rapport with Kassandra through more than a dozen video sessions. While she remained mostly shy and quiet, I was satisfied she didn't seem to view me as just another adult telling her what not to do—or if she did, it wasn't enough to end our dialogue. By sharing some of my own troubled past, we found ways to relate to each other through our ideological experiences. I made a connection and, I hoped, planted a seed for a future that remained open, that would liberate her from the manacles of hate, if she chose it.

I explained to Kassandra's parents that even with their daughter's high intelligence, she was so enamored with Bergsson and convinced of his affection for her that it clouded her ability to see what she was involved in. To wake her up, I suggested walking Kassandra through an exhibit of evidence I was collecting on Bergsson to poke holes in his fraudulent identity.

"I've found some originals of the doctored videos and photos he sent to Kassandra," I said, "and I'm building a solid dossier. But I need more time. I know Bergsson is a fraud but I don't know who is behind it yet." In the meantime, I recommended they document anything more they turned up so we could present it to Kassandra together in person. They agreed, and for the next four weeks the three of us uncovered all we could about who was behind the fake Jakob Bergsson alias.

It was an intense month of investigation and research. Between Kassandra's parents and me, we collected every phony bit of information she had ever received from her boyfriend, including a supposed home address. Everything Bergsson told Kassandra was a lie.

Unbeknownst to her, Jack and Meredith installed web-tracking software on their home network to make sure Kassandra honored their Internet access restrictions. Although it was a dictate she often defied, it was to our advantage. Everything Bergsson sent her was also coming to me to decipher. The photos, social media accounts, email addresses, and the throwaway phone number Kassandra's parents saw her engaged with nearly every waking hour, were fake. Stolen, doctored, burners, or untraceable—all of them.

With the invaluable help of Meredith—who went from protective mother to savvy web sleuth in just a month—I followed every digital lead through a sordid labyrinth of unadulterated hate and a dark web of drug and weapons sales, fetish pornography, extremist propaganda in online message boards, and tens of thousands of politically charged, fake social media accounts run by human trolls and Twitter bots—artificially intelligent Internet applications that can engage in "real" conversations with unsuspecting users. To avoid detection by Bergsson's many online identities—or "sock puppet" accounts—I mirrored his tactics and created several covert, "Nazi-friendly" sock puppets of my own. To follow him, I registered accounts on every platform where he lurked, including Twitter, YouTube, Facebook, 4chan, and Stormfront.

Bergsson's various online accounts were all tied together. His social media profiles included two common elements that sometimes overlapped: he claimed Eagle, Idaho, as his home (though public records show no one named Bergsson on the tax roll in the entire state), and all the accounts were linked to one of two email addresses used to communicate with Kassandra. Aside from the blatant pro-Nazi and *Make America Great Again* motifs on all the bogus profiles, nothing else seemed out of place. But as I dug deeper and analyzed the various accounts, one of his common followers caught my attention: a "friend" listed as living in Moscow, Russia.

So, I pulled at the thread.

Based on a matching screen name I found for the Moscow account on the social media site VK—the Russian equivalent of Facebook—and another hit on a Russian-language web forum, I discovered evidence showing at least one person behind the Bergsson alias was a Russian named Maksim Volkov. Volkov had also used Bergsson's email to set up an old MySpace account—decidedly not a coincidence.

Volkov appeared in online photos looking as I imagined a stereotypical millennial in Moscow might. He was flashy, wearing a royal-blue sharkskin suit to the discotheque; a lover of video games who also enjoyed soccer in the park with his mates; and he drove a shiny, brand-new white Mercedes sedan. His public VK and MySpace profiles didn't appear current, which meant one of two things: the lead would end up proving worthless—a coincidence—or could offer new clues.

It proved to be the latter.

I learned Volkov was a graduate of the University of Moscow with an advanced degree in English and German linguistics—the languages Bergsson spoke with Kassandra—and he'd served in the Russian Signal Corps. The puzzle formed a telling picture: tech savvy, trained in military communications, and fluent in multiple languages—the profile of a Russian FSB intelligence officer. I forwarded screen grabs of what I found to Meredith.

Kassandra's situation had spiraled into something even more bewildering than the potential sex-trafficking ring I initially pegged it as. If Russian intelligence was involved—as I now suspected they were—this had crossed over into the realm of national security. It sounded so unlikely that I worried about my own mental state, let alone how others might see me after explaining the craziness of what I found. Decades had passed for me since conspiracies lurked behind every glance or spoken word, and as I pulled at the frayed edges of the elaborate tapestry of Jakob Bergsson, I wondered if I lost my mind again as I had at fourteen.

I kept careful notes and organized files on every new lead I turned up, hoping my hunch about national security implications would amount to nothing.

By now, Bergsson had set up a fraudulent online fundraising account in Kassandra's name. With credentials she naïvely handed over at the beginning of their relationship, he was impersonating her and raised several hundred dollars by alleging to her followers that their donations would resurrect the Valkyrie Vixen video channel her parents had by now taken offline. Meredith and I linked three more Facebook profiles to at least one other previously confirmed data point from the primary Jakob Bergsson alias, all with variations of the name: *Jake BergSSon; Jacob LarSSon; Jakob WeiSS;* plus, a handful of YouTube accounts and more than thirty Twitter handles using variations of *Jakob* and surnames that emphasized an uppercase *SS*, which paid subtle tribute to the Schutzstaffel, or the SS—Adolf Hitler's personal murder squad.

I also found other young girls Bergsson had victimized—some who were in his grip for years. They appeared to be in their mid-to-late teens and resembled Kassandra in appearance. All of them similarly groomed into being neo-Nazi propagandists on YouTube. These earlier attempts by Bergsson were less polished versions of the mouthpiece he had created in Kassandra. But the technique was the same: an attractive, well-spoken, white girl reading a script on camera, teeming with provocative Nazi imagery, one-sided talk about the greatness of white Europeans, fearmongering, and anti-Semitic conspiracies. The production quality of the videos improved over time, but the narratives, plot twists, and leading actresses were too alike to ignore.

According to a text message that accompanied the most recent photo Bergsson had sent of his new campus quad at Boise State University, he claimed to be pursuing an undergraduate degree in architecture. A quick search of the school's website showed it offered no architectural program or related courses. Upon intercepting his photo, Kassandra's parents took away her mobile phone, which Meredith had only recently granted restricted access to after discovering Bergsson's plea for her underage daughter to send nude selfies. A week after Meredith's confiscation, a package containing a replacement prepaid phone for Kassandra, with no sign that a carrier service shipped the package, was left at their front door—inside their gated community.

The gift came with a simple typed note that read: *For my beautiful Valkyrie, from your lonely wolf. XOXO and Heil Hitler—Jakob.*

That stunt was enough for Meredith and Jack to call the police. Although the detective assigned to the case seemed genuinely concerned after they explained the sordid details of the case, I knew where these kinds of slow-burn "Internet stalking" and "online bullying" situations—that's how the authorities classified it—fell in the stack of priorities for a busy local police department. I expected little if any of their help. The detective asked Jack and Meredith to keep her updated, "should anything new and more concrete develop."

I didn't have the slightest clue at the time how deep everything went, but I knew enough to concern me. There were solid connections between the mysterious Jakob Bergsson persona and the alt-right, online influence campaigns targeting the upcoming election, and a Russian spy agency. When I accepted I was in over my head and veering toward danger, I reached out to law enforcement and called on a friendly FBI contact that I advised on terrorist interventions in the past. No one's safety was worth jeopardizing, let alone that of our democracy.

The FBI, however, did not appear too concerned or even remotely interested in what I found. A bitter disappointment, but not the first time the federal government failed to recognize the threat of homegrown violent extremism. And, sadly, not the last time Americans would pay the consequences for their failure to do so.

# 6

## Extremist Recruitment

### *Reggie*

A WEEK AFTER THE 9/11 TRAGEDY, Reggie ran into the recruiter's office on his eighteenth birthday to enlist in the United States Marine Corps. He didn't sign up because he hated or wanted to kill Muslims— he didn't know any. Instead, Reggie wanted to be part of something important, to serve his country and do something great with his miserable life. America was the only thing he had left in the world to care about. He craved being able to do something he could be proud of. Even if one wrong decision came after the next throughout Reggie's entire existence, something worth saving inside of him had to exist. No matter how bad a hand life dealt him, he was sure his luck would turn.

Reggie didn't have to venture out far to hit potholes in life. Growing up in Buffalo, New York, in an abusive family, they appeared early on.

His mother's embattled upbringing by an abusive widower had left her with little ability to discern for herself that the man she fell in love with was, in the words of her own wretched father, a "nasty son of a bitch." Her husband was an abusive drinker like her father had been. Reggie's mother stayed in the relationship because she feared her husband's wrath if she ever tried to leave. To cope, she drank, mixing her first martini of the day at 3:00 p.m. before he got home from work, every day since she got pregnant at eighteen with Reggie. Another cocktail followed every hour on the hour until she passed out. Painkillers also worked as advertised—they helped kill his mother's pain, physically and emotionally. Growing up, Reggie wished he could help her somehow, but he was no match for his punchy father's stone knuckles.

Violence and disorder were unpleasant facts for Reggie as a kid. He told me early in our relationship that the only memories he had of his parents together were of him curled up on the couch hiding under a blanket, trying to tune out his blitzed father as he beat the daylights out of his mom for leaving dirty dishes in the sink or whatever else he decided she'd done wrong that day.

After his dad died in a drunk driving accident where he wrapped his pickup around a light post, Reggie's mother fell so deep into opioid addiction that when Reggie dropped out of high school during his second year, she didn't notice.

He skimmed pills from his mom's stash, but they weren't enough to calm his angry impulses and hyperactivity—so he found a friend in heroin. Reggie drank more than his father ever had. He'd started at the age of nine after his dad challenged him to chug a twelve-ounce can of Pabst Blue Ribbon at dinner, which soon became their nightly bonding ritual. By eleven, it was straight whiskey. In his teens, it was a rarity to see Reggie without a flask pressed to his lips.

He knew the other kids in the neighborhood lived different lives, but they never invited him over, so he couldn't be sure. Reggie pretended not to care, even if he felt his father had shamed the family. At first, the junk he shot into his arm quieted his secret longing to be "normal" like the families he admired in the sitcoms and made-for-TV movies he lost himself in to escape real life, but now, the drugs just made him feel hopeless—no matter how much he injected into his veins or snorted.

When the Twin Towers fell, eighteen-year-old Reggie heard a calling to do something meaningful. He hadn't been able to save his mother from his father's brutality, or his father from the bottle, but he'd do his damnedest to protect his country. And war? He wasn't afraid. He had seen it in the movies with all its guts and gore. Violence was nothing new to Reggie. It was in his DNA. He was his father's son after all. This time, he thought, being on the right side of things, maybe he could break the family curse.

Reggie had few friends growing up. In the three years after he dropped out of high school and got himself clean and enlisted, the ones he kept in contact with took turns dying from overdoses—each of them gone before their twenty-first birthdays.

His fellow soldiers became the brothers he always wanted. Marines had one another's back—it was in their code of conduct. Everybody wore the same uniform. It didn't matter where you lived or how often the cops came to your house for a wellness check. In the military, Reggie was part of what felt to him like a real, functioning family, a big one with a sacred role: protecting the Homeland.

One of the first friends Reggie made in basic training was a young skinhead from Pittsburgh. Their friendship blossomed through a shared love of punk music. Reggie found solace from his tumultuous upbringing in punk rock, though the brand of gutter punk he enjoyed was more about scorched earth philosophy than protest. It was this new friend's white-power music that caught Reggie's attention and became his new drug of choice. It was raucous, lean, unabashed, organized chaos, he thought. The songs screamed the word *faggot* more than his father had, something he didn't think was possible, but somehow found comforting in its familiarity. The hard-driving music and the pointed lyrics of this style of hate rock spoke to Reggie and drew him into a world where toughness won, and people were reducible to black and white foes locked in a death match.

Reggie was near the end of his basic training in 2002 when he heard the news of the last of his friends back home dying. He was despondent but grateful he would avoid the same fate, now with a tribe of his own to support him. Then everything changed. He tore his knee up badly in a hand-to-hand combat exercise. The Marine Corps had little choice but to present Reggie with a general discharge and send him home. As his fellow marines, young men he now called brothers—the first close friends he ever knew—deployed to Afghanistan, Reggie took off his uniform and fell back into civilian life. He kept his service benefits but got neither the glory nor the sense of purpose he went in craving.

His skinhead pal reminded him there was plenty for him to do outside of the military. He shared names and contact numbers and connected Reggie with "brothers" who were "doing good stuff."

Reggie pursued his passion for music by starting a racist music mail-order business. What began for him as a personal collection—an obsession, really—turned into a business venture. He sold white-power music and reproduction Nazi-era patches through a website and a printed catalog that he mailed to like-minded people, and he made enough money to scrape by. The music was propaganda that surged with incitements to violence, something I knew all too well. Reggie didn't see it that way, though. He felt he could do what he hadn't been able to do in the military—fight for the homeland. The enemy? Muslims. He was getting other whites to open their eyes and join the cause through the music he sold. Maybe he wasn't fighting brown-skinned terrorists with assault weapons in far-off lands, but he was arming the white race with the knowledge they needed to destroy the enemy here at home. For Reggie, at least in the short term, that seemed just as good.

Reggie is not the first or only person to become radicalized into extremism out of a genuine belief they were doing something righteous. He figured out ways to mask his potholes—mainly through substance abuse and the denial it sometimes fed—so he was not necessarily vulnerable for those reasons. He didn't set out to find a radical political movement to figure out who he was either—though the ideology did conceal his low self-esteem. With his life in shambles, and because Reggie believed others saw him as a loser, it put him at risk of becoming radicalized given the right context. When he committed himself to service in the wake of a national tragedy and then found himself unable to complete it, Reggie's desire to prove himself became his undoing.

Gullible and desperate, Reggie bought the white nationalism pitch his friend sold him.

His desire to "get things right" led him straight into the insidious arms of hate. His strong desire to repair the fractured world in front of him swung the door wide open for anyone with an unscrupulous agenda to walk through. Extremists understand that someone who desperately wants to make a difference—who has found few if any outlets for their idealism—is someone more easily led in the wrong direction, often without a great deal of prodding. For someone who has had difficulty finding acceptance in a peer group or who feels worthless or powerless, a sudden invitation to participate in something of almost mythological significance, to save a group of people—a race—from annihilation from the face of the planet, can seem an extraordinary honor. That's how Reggie saw it.

Reggie's troubled profile is typical of an extremist recruiter's targets. While extremists would have followers believe their radical movements seek the elite of their "kind," the opposite is true.

Few environments where violence plays a significant role are composed of happy, whole, or well-adjusted people. In my eight years as a neo-Nazi skinhead, and in the more than two decades following my disengagement, I have not met one emotionally "healthy" extremist who remains active. That's not to say there are not friendly, polite, and seemingly "normal" people who moonlight as hate-spewing bigots behind closed doors and computer monitors, but every single extremist I've ever met was dealing with an ICP crisis and serious unresolved potholes. For most of those same individuals, their significant underlying trauma had gone ignored for years, sometimes an entire lifetime. Manipulative extremists—who are themselves deeply broken individuals—understand that where communities of alienated people gather, some will do anything to find acceptance. They see it as an opportunity to lure marginalized, road-weary seekers of ICP with empty promises of glory.

Aware that prospective recruits need social connection, extremists play on the language of family, calling on "brothers and sisters" to join their fight. The camaraderie felt while fighting for a cause with high stakes cements the familial bond. A culture of extremism is often presented as warm and welcoming, even empowering, to new recruits. Only those fortunate enough to have seen through the deceit that once blinded them can fully appreciate that within these movements it is truly every man or woman for themselves—and the only real enemies that ever existed were ourselves and those we were conditioned to trust.

# 7

## A Mental Health Crisis

### *Kassandra*

I WORKED ALONGSIDE KASSANDRA'S PARENTS FOR a month in cyberspace and over the phone before I found the chance to meet them in person, something I try to do with all the people I help. Finally, on a trip to New York to film my documentary television series, *Breaking Hate,* the opportunity presented itself. Before catching a bus to their house in bucolic Teaneck, New Jersey, I found a print shop and assembled the intelligence brief I had gathered on Jakob Bergsson.

I was looking forward to exposing at least one of the criminals behind their daughter's torment, but even more so to meeting the people who had become like family to me.

Meredith greeted me at the front door with a warm embrace and a hot mug of coffee when I arrived. A few minutes later, Jack emerged from his den wearing a houndstooth blazer and corduroy slippers. He gripped my hand and shook it for what seemed like too long, like he didn't want to let go. After what the family had been going through with Kassandra, it was heartening to finally meet them.

I looked forward to getting some face time with Kassandra and continuing to build a rapport between us, but forty minutes after I arrived, she still hadn't elected to join us in the kitchen.

When Kassandra finally emerged from the safety of her bedroom, I rose from my seat at the kitchen table to meet her. She had huge deep-set eyes that were unsmiling and inscrutable. Pale and thin, Kassandra appeared fragile, like a delicate porcelain heirloom. She wore her long black hair the same way it appeared in her YouTube videos. The scent of acrid perfume—like something you'd smell in an old folks' home—wafted from her. Her button-down shirt matched the black of every other bit of clothing she wore, something I could relate to.

She looked around at each of us, studying our outlines as if we were holding loaded dueling pistols behind our backs. I took a gentle step toward her and extended my hand from a few feet away, aware that she saw me as an obstacle to her true love. She flinched when I approached, and I worried she might flee back to her room. But she steadied herself and raised her delicate hand to meet my outstretched palm. Almost soundlessly, she slid down into a straight-back chair opposite me and her parents at the kitchen table.

I gleaned a lot about Kassandra's volatile emotional state from her parents before speaking directly with her over video chat. Besides feeling betrayed and abandoned by her identical twin, Simone, and blaming the giggling schoolgirls as the wedge that forced its way between them, Kassandra was very uncomfortable in groups of people. It panicked her. She was also unable to make sense of popular references—she'd never heard of Lady Gaga—and couldn't engage even when others embraced her.

During the four weeks I video-chatted with Kassandra before meeting, her behavior grew concerning, sometimes turning violent. When she didn't get her way, Kassandra threw things—once, it was a pair of scissors from the kitchen drawer hurled at her father. Another time, she jabbed him in the forearm with a pen, and during a particularly intense argument over computer curfew she threatened to stab Meredith with a steak knife. Other times, Kassandra became withdrawn to the point of being unreachable.

Facing her across the table, I attempted some friendly banter, but Kassandra responded only in clipped monosyllables. Despite her lack of social maturity, she was precocious, using words that might have been more at home in the mouth of a seventy-year-old matron than a girl of seventeen. Between sentences, she seemed to find her cuticles more interesting than my small talk.

After trying in vain to ease into the conversation, I realized my subtle approach was counterproductive. Kassandra shut me out. Shaking her reluctance to engage would take something bolder. Pondering a course of action, I considered the aggression she showed toward her parents and the violence she advocated for in her videos, wondering if she cultivated her fragile appearance with deliberation, both to disarm and deceive.

I jumped straight to Bergsson. "Kassandra, do you know why I'm here?" I asked twice before getting her attention. Unlike the confident young woman who outlined her thesis on the "White European Struggle Against International Jewry" with vigor in her video invectives, the flesh-and-bones Kassandra kept her gaze averted, uncomfortable communicating. She smiled at times, but with vacancy in her eyes.

Meredith reached over to top off my coffee, filling the dead air with a fresh aroma.

"Kassandra, honey," Jack broke in, "like we mentioned, we reached out to Christian for help with your—with *our* situation," he said, adjusting himself to sound like the meeting was a team endeavor.

"I know, Dad," Kassandra mumbled back in a low monotone, attempting to end the awkward exchange.

"Kassandra, your parents contacted me," I said, "because your safety concerns them. We've discovered some things about your friend Jakob Bergsson." I reached for the file I assembled, then caught myself, leaving it for later in the conversation. "I hope you don't think I'm here to talk you out of being a National Socialist."

Her fingers stopped picking at her nail beds, and she raised her round, aquamarine eyes to meet mine. I opted to use what Nazis consider the proper term for their ideological persuasion as a sign of respect for Kassandra—not to pay respect to her ideology. I knew that no Nazi liked being called a Nazi, especially if someone used it as a general label like *bigot* or *racist* to brand them as a hater.

When I told Kassandra about my experiences in the movement when I was her age, she started to unfold a bit and moved beyond the dismissive grunts that were her initial responses. She shared insight into her interests in medieval English literature and European classical music, her love for Wagner's "Ride of the Valkyries," and the out-of-context Nietzsche passages I'd also memorized at seventeen. None of her pro-white pabulum came as a surprise. After I attempted to slip in a bad dad joke about trading my old Doc Martens for orthopedic boots, I sensed Kassandra—a bright and talented young lady—would not respond to humor. Not because I wasn't being particularly funny, which was doubtless the case, but because she couldn't recognize irony.

I also observed that Kassandra's responses, however brief, had grown heady beyond what I would expect to see in a shy teenager confronted by an adult. When she allowed us to hear her opinions, she became unyielding, viewing situations as strictly black and white with no room in between. I could see how the rigidity of an authoritarian ideology and an adherence to traditionalism and fundamentalism might appeal to her. The routine and structure of her extremist ideology, as opposed to the randomness of life, was comforting for her.

Kassandra's ability to hyper-focus and absorb information, if not the nuances that help most of us to make sense of it, made her an expert in Nazi lore, policy, and statistics in no time. At seventeen, she knew it better than most seasoned old-school movement folk I'd ever met. But she had no sense of the historical human tragedy her beliefs caused—and she lacked empathy for its victims. In her mind, the horror of six million Jewish lives lost in the Holocaust didn't happen. It was a hoax she refused to believe. The gravity of it neither registered emotionally nor gave her pause.

Even though discussing ideology—which I generally try to avoid in my disengagement work—had drawn her out, Kassandra's eyes glazed over when I turned the subject back to her online videos and her continued involvement with Bergsson. She had no interest, it seemed, in discussing anything but her ideology. Unwilling to take her bait, I instead peppered her with questions about what she wanted to communicate in her videos and how she started making them. Jack and Meredith grew quiet, shifting in their seats, fearful we hit a wall.

"Let me get you more coffee, dear," Meredith said. She returned to me with the pot and added a splash to my mug, which remained full.

As Kassandra reverted to answering my questions with cagey responses, our meeting seemed like it was headed for failure. I decided it was time; I had no choice but to lay Bergsson's twenty-six-page dossier out in front of everyone.

I dug up dozens of solid leads, most of which led me in circles without a clear answer to the mystery of who Jakob Bergsson was or on whose behalf he'd been catfishing girls like Kassandra. His social media posts pointed to his status as a seasoned Nazi, but the abundance of Russian troll accounts I found him linked to left me baffled. Was the interest in Kassandra to recruit her into white supremacy, or was this a sexual predator situation? Even if the answers around the Russian angle proved elusive, I felt I had gathered enough concrete and revealing information to shock Kassandra's system.

I walked the family through my time line, highlighting the links between the copious amounts of media I archived. I presented them with Bergsson's altered photographs—the one's he'd stolen to pass off to Kassandra as his own—and I contrasted them with the unedited originals he ripped from the websites of two unsuspecting European male models. I played video clips of the Aryan-looking twentysomething Bergsson had sent to Kassandra as his own personal love notes. I followed them with their undoctored versions, which Bergsson pilfered from a British YouTuber and manipulated to suit his needs. He had stripped the audio tracks from the original files and recorded his own poetic messages—both in German and English—matching his words to the lip movements of his newly inhabited body. They were hack jobs and easily identifiable as fakes to her parents and me but had blown right through Kassandra's filter—as did all the manipulated photos he sent, which weren't as easy to spot.

I briefly touched on his sex forum postings, the solicitation by one of the Bergsson alias accounts to buy and sell illicit drugs on the dark web, and the spiderweb of fraudulent identities he'd spun across dozens of websites and platforms.

I burned an entire month trying to unmask Jakob Bergsson, finding myself more invested in Kassandra's safety with each lurid clue. I drove home the dishonesty of Bergsson's manipulation like a concerned parent and stressed the danger of a potential sex-trafficking ring. I explained there were other female victims and that his Idaho home address was fake. Talking to the real homeowner confirmed it.

Rising from his seat, Jack coughed, choking on his coffee, while Meredith comforted him with pats on his back. When he regained normal breathing and relaxed into his chair, Jack and Meredith locked eyes, then turned to Kassandra. They looked like a bus hit them. Kassandra shook her head in disbelief. She cleared her throat, and suddenly her voice came out loud and distinct. "No, you're wrong," she said, "you're lying to me." According to Kassandra, I was using fabrications to destroy her only source of joy. I was belittling and attacking the only person she believed had ever loved her. Jakob Bergsson, Kassandra thought, was not scheming to dupe her but was instead her white knight in shining armor saving her from a world gone foul.

After Kassandra's passionate defense of her boyfriend, she sat in silence, head down with her long black hair covering her face.

I wanted to scream at her to snap out of it, to tell her she was not just perpetrating horrible lies about people who experienced far more misfortune than she ever had but that she was being selfish, too, putting herself and her family at risk.

I was starting to lose focus, vignettes of my own misspent youth flashing before me. I thought about the others who found themselves lost in extremist movements and reached out to me, new emails lining my in-box each day like prayers of mercy. Would any of those people be more receptive or a better use of my energy? I shook it off, reassuring myself that nobody's disengagement was easy and this young girl and her family needed me.

Jack and Meredith were silent, hands clasped in each other's as they scanned the pages of notes and studied the ripples in their coffee mugs for answers, avoiding their daughter's eyes.

A car double-honked in the driveway. We turned in unison to see my taxi outside the kitchen window. I glanced at my watch, surprised by the time. Fearing I might be late for my flight to Brussels, I gathered my papers together into my folder and pushed my chair back, apologizing for needing to leave in a hurry. I extended my hand to Kassandra, who ignored it. I promised to visit again soon.

Meredith and Jack rose along with me, and Meredith shot me a sympathetic glance. She had become accustomed to Kassandra's behavior and thought it best not to confront her daughter over it just then, given our delicate balancing act.

At the door, I slipped Meredith my dossier on Bergsson. "Keep this safe," I added. She frowned, and I nodded. I knew she understood the unspoken words: *safe from Kassandra.* Jack put his arm around my shoulder and hugged me.

Meredith then handed me the latest Bergsson intercept. I hugged her and folded the printout, shoving it into the front pocket of my backpack. I knew Jack and Meredith were nursing some harsh blows, and I assured them they were two of the strongest people and some of the most devoted parents I had ever met.

"We'll find the end of this together," I said, waving goodbye.

On my way to the airport, I reflected on the encounter with Kassandra. Her decisive behavior, after hearing the damning truth behind Jakob Bergsson, stuck out to me more than her words. Her shift in demeanor was the only genuine emotion I saw from her the entire time we were together. She was distant, unable to establish eye contact, difficult to engage in playful conversation, and expressed no visible concern for how her decisions impacted others. She took my jokes literally or missed them altogether. It wasn't just because of her awkwardness. I knew these were potential signs of an emotional problem or even a psychological disorder but I had rushed out before bringing my concerns to Meredith or Jack. If we were going to move forward in helping Kassandra, we would need to have a potentially difficult conversation first.

Now that I met Kassandra, I saw that the marginalizing factors surrounding her mental health—alienation, anxiety, and stigmatization—which had gone undiagnosed and untreated, were contributing factors to her radicalization. I felt it was imperative that her parents involved a psychiatric professional to get a proper diagnosis.

I called Meredith and explained my concern. I was nervous, fully aware I wasn't qualified to provide a clinical diagnosis and that no parent wants to hear that their child may be struggling with their mental health. When I built up enough courage and dialed her number, Meredith's calm reply relieved me. She understood I only wanted to help her daughter. "I think it's best to rule everything out," I said. "Kassandra might be dealing with something she doesn't know anything about. If she is, she needs to learn how to manage living with it."

When Jack and Meredith told Kassandra she would be seeing a psychologist, she raged against their decision. They called on a special unit of the local police department, one they'd sought beforehand to help mitigate any future abusive eruptions from their daughter. Led by police officers trained in mental health and social work, the team made clear to Kassandra they would handle her with compassion. She cooperated, and they transported her without incident to the local hospital for a seventy-two-hour psychological evaluation.

It resulted in a diagnosis that identified some specific conditions, including autism spectrum disorder (ASD), that the family could finally address.

It was one of the first signs of a significant trend I could no longer ignore—a high prevalence of autism-related disorders affecting almost three out of every four extremists I work with. Because it is so common, I now ask everyone to consider seeing a psychologist or a professional counselor as an early step in our relationship.

With this revelation about Kassandra, we now understood the extent to which she had struggled in her coming of age. Mental health does not discriminate by income or social status and is one of the many reasons someone with seemingly endless possibilities from a loving, stable family can become drawn to a hateful narrative that falsely promises healthy notions of ICP they may not otherwise experience in the real world.

Kassandra's parents believed she would grow out of her shyness and become less clumsy as she got older, but without professional guidance to help decipher her complex emotions and how her perception of the world diverged from others her age, Kassandra never learned how to embrace what made her unique. So, over time, her bond with society broke down. Other children may very well have teased Kassandra as "odd" during her youth, and unable to figure out why—to Kassandra, these children teasing her seemed odd—she instead created a dense expanse around herself to make her isolation complete. Her disconnection and lifelong conditioning of alienation and uncertainty—her pre-radicalization potholes—sent her stumbling down the path toward extremism.

Kassandra latched onto Jakob Bergsson's notion of who was invading her safety because it provided her with a sense of clarity as to why she felt uneasy her entire life. When she met Bergsson, the one person in the world who seemed capable of understanding her pain, Kassandra nestled into his foxhole—she belonged to him, she decided—and dug herself in to protect her wounds from an outside world she saw as hostile.

A childhood marked by feelings of isolation taught Kassandra all the wrong lessons about how to thrive with a condition that could have set her apart. Instead of identifying the source of her pain and grappling with how her differences might become assets instead of impediments, she looked for the source of her agony elsewhere. Without knowing why life felt this way, Kassandra adapted to the harsh reality, believing life was supposed to be painful and confusing, as she holed up in her bedroom for survival. She never learned how to share her feelings, nor was she ever taught it was okay to ask for help—and no one ever thought to ask her how she felt.

The Internet became Kassandra's lifeline.

There, she transformed herself into Valkyrie Vixen, a powerful voice that spoke to the issues of her time, who was worthy of respect and glory—she was not broken.

It must be said that millions of people who live—and thrive—with mental health–related conditions similar to or more serious than Kassandra's will never travel down a path toward extremism. A psychological disorder doesn't cause someone to become racist, nor does a mental health condition directly predispose people to accept an extremist ideology. Rather, the feelings of alienation and uncertainty that often accompany mental health conditions and isolating social anxieties are what can drive people to the fringes. Without the strength of a trusted community or mental health professionals to steer would-be extremists away from the fallacies of their hatred, the consolation provided by the black-and-white thinking of fiery ideologues can be difficult to resist. Like shame, marginalization relegates people to the peripheries where sharp narratives can sometimes provide false hope for those who feel hopeless.

Clare Allely, a researcher at the Gillberg Neuropsychiatry Centre at the University of Gothenburg in Sweden, clarifies the connection:

*It is important to caution…there is no substantial link between autism spectrum disorder and terrorism. However, there are specific risk factors which could increase the risk of offending among people with ASD. Autistic special interests such as fantasy, obsessiveness (extreme compulsiveness), the need for routine and predictability, and social communication difficulties all increase the vulnerability of a person with ASD to going down the pathway to terrorism.\**

As my taxi pulled up to the curb of the airport terminal, my phone buzzed inside my pocket. It was my wife, Britton.

"Hi, honey," I answered. "Can I call you back in a few minutes, once I get through security?"

She was silent for a moment. "Sure," she said, "but look at your website first."

When I checked, I saw that someone had hacked my website. Malicious code injected by hackers now treated unsuspecting visitors who clicked on the contact form—where they can summon help—to an array of pornographic ads with explicit multiracial themes.

The intermittent Wi-Fi on my long flight to Brussels gave me a few opportunities to shore up my digital defenses, but I spent most of my transatlantic prison term vacillating between feelings of frustration and rage. Sitting helpless in economy class, it felt like the entire diseased contents of a Third Reich latrine bubbled up and flowed into my space.

Anonymous accounts began posting defamatory statements about me on social media. Videos calling me an Israeli Mossad agent, a

---

\* C. Allely, "Are Autistic People at Greater Risk of Being Radicalised?," *Conversation*, June 22, 2017, accessed August 8, 2019, https://theconversation.com/are-autistic-people-at-greater-risk -of-being-radicalised-76726/.

paid FBI informant, and an "antiwhite hate-monger" sprouted up on YouTube and message boards across the Internet. My wife received intimidating messages claiming I was a child rapist, and someone who impersonated my son called my mother later that evening and nearly convinced her to divulge my private phone number.

I had become public enemy number one to the World Wide Web of white nationalism. Given the timing, just hours after meeting with Kassandra and revealing who, as far as I could tell, Bergsson was, it left little doubt about who was responsible. Kassandra had leaked the information I presented. She told Bergsson what I knew and he unleashed his digital assassins in a retaliatory strike.

I puzzled over how, even with Bergsson's sprawling web of troll accounts, he could have coordinated an attack on this scale so fast. I knew the alt-right's online communities were potent and could orchestrate spontaneous spam attacks and harassment but they seemed too diffuse to attack in as technical, swift, and coordinated a way as this. It was a digital swarm on a scale I hadn't yet seen from a neo-Nazi group online. It convinced me that powerful outside influences were buffeting American white supremacy's sudden online growth.

My head whirled, trying to make sense of the ominous possibilities.

As I stowed my laptop before touching down in Brussels, the note I received from Meredith before leaving the house fell from my backpack to the cabin floor.

I unfolded the printout, revealing Bergsson's most recent message intended for Kassandra. This one written in German: *Triff mich in Tr3nt0n, meine Liebe, und lass uns verschwinden. Ich werde das datum und den ort per verschlüsseltem chat senden. Nur du und ich. Machen wir einen Dylann Roof in ganz Amerika.*

I pulled my computer back out of my backpack and quickly logged on again as the plane descended. Before losing the Wi-Fi connection, I typed Bergsson's words into my browser, swapping *Trenton* for *Tr3nt0n*, what I assumed was alphanumeric code for the New Jersey city where Kassandra lived.

The translation that came back left me feeling certain I mistyped it. As I tried again in another translation tool hoping to correct my error, a flight attendant reminded me—first politely and then sternly as I nodded, asking for just one minute—to power down.

Bergsson's words came back the same: *Meet me in Trenton, my love, and let's disappear. I will send the date and location via encrypted chat. Just you and me. Let's do a Dylann Roof across America.*

# 8

---

## Toxic Masculinity

### *Dallas*

*N*EED HELP. *ABT* IS HOLDING ME AGAINST MY WILL.

Her first text message came in at 7:04 on a rare lazy Sunday morning while my wife and I were sleeping. After Britton nudged me, which meant she didn't appreciate being woken by the sound of my phone, I reached over to silence it and check the message, wondering who would text this early on a weekend.

After rubbing the sleep from my eyes, I still couldn't recognize the number on my screen. But when I read the message, I learned it met the requirement for getting me out of bed.

I tapped furiously on my phone: *This is Christian. What's your name?*

Radio silence.

*Are you safe and can you tell me where you are?*

Sitting on the edge of my bed, I hoped this was another trolling incident by a Nazi nuisance with too much time and not enough courage to ask me for help in a more direct way. It was just like them to target my weakness: sleep.

Britton followed me out of bed. "Is everything okay, honey?"

"I'm not sure. It's a text message. Probably nothing, just a bored troll. You should go back to bed, sweetheart."

I knew the ABT acronym in the text message referred to the Aryan Brotherhood of Texas, a civilian dotted line to the notorious Aryan

Brotherhood prison outfit. On the streets, ABT operated more like a criminal enterprise focused on drug and sex trafficking, racketeering, and murder than as ideological extremists, though it was no secret which radical belief system they pledged allegiance to. If this message was real, it was deadly serious. I wasn't willing to guess wrong with someone's life in the balance—even if it meant only five hours of sleep and spending my Sunday morning serving breakfast to a troll.

Then the first photo came in, followed by another. I found both difficult to stomach.

Strewn across an oil-stained concrete garage floor appeared to be articles of women's clothing—a lone shoe, crumpled panties, a torn halter top—and shards of broken glass. The second image was more shadowy, barely revealing the front end of an old powder-blue passenger van and two digits from its license plate. On the windshield, I made out a faded decal in the shape of the Lone Star State.

My pulse quickened, and my back bolted upright. The Texas sticker made sense given the ABT reference. I doubted a troll would bother with that level of deceptive detail.

A burst of rapid-fire texts came in furious succession.

*The man who owns me said I know too much.*

*I am their property now.*

*Took one of their phones last night after one guy blacked out.*

*Gave up hope of getting away weeks ago. Not in a safe place. One man passed out in the room with me. Other men here in building I think.*

*Help me.*

"Britton," I shouted over the coffee grinder my wife was using in the kitchen as I mimed putting a phone against my ear. "I need your phone!"

The grinder stopped, leaving a disquieting blankness in the air. "What's going on?"

"I need you to Google this phone number," I said, firing off the digits on my screen, hoping to find a public match.

*OK,* I typed to the woman. *I understand. I will help. Can you get out safely if I send someone to pick you up?*

*Scared to move right now,* she replied.

*Where are you? City or address?*

*Somewhere near Dallas in a garage or repair shop. That's all I know.*

I threw on the nearest clothes I could find. I appreciated the full stakes of this woman's situation—if her captors caught her texting me, she would end up dead.

*I need your help, okay?* I texted. *Do you see something or can you remember anything that might tell me where you are?*

After a few minutes, her third and final photo came in. This time it was a clear snapshot of a stack of envelopes—mail with names and addresses.

*Perfect! Stand by.*

Britton joined me in our home office as I switched between logging on to my laptop and inexplicably glaring at the messages on my phone.

"Looks like the number is to a body shop in Fort Worth, Texas," Britton reported. "Why? What's going on?"

"I'm not sure. This woman texting me says she is being held against her will, and I think she's in danger."

When I enlarged the image on my phone, the stack of mail turned out to be a bundle of bank statement envelopes. On top, the recipient's Fort Worth address was unmistakable—as was a business name.

*I know where you are. Will call police.*

*NO! They will kill me,* she shot back in a hurry. *Scared. Drugs and guns here. I think it involves cops.*

She was right to be afraid. A group like the ABT wouldn't take a breach like this lightly if it compromised an operation and meant jail time. If she was also correct about police involvement, it meant I couldn't look to the local cops for help.

Now that I had this information, I also feared my family might become targets.

*OK. If I can get someone I trust to pick you up, would you be willing to try to get outside?*

While waiting for her reply, I scrambled on my computer to search for a colleague's phone number in my email. Her next message came five minutes later, after what seemed a lifetime.

*If they wake up now, I'm dead.*

I called a colleague in the Civil Rights Division at Homeland Security whom I had met at several counter-extremism conferences and developed a cordial relationship with. He picked up right away and put me in touch with an FBI contact in Dallas.

*I have a solution, but you need to be brave.*

*OK but scared. Please be for real. I don't want to die here.*

Though I was flying blind and unsure of the scenario, I would not let any harm come to this woman. I couldn't promise her that but I did. *It will be okay. What's your name?*

*They call me Dallas,* she demurred.

*All right, Dallas. I need you to tell me when you think you're clear on the inside to move. After I get your go-ahead, I'll text that your pizza is ready for pickup when it's time to make for the door. You will need to move quietly but quickly. Exit the front of the building and turn right. A black SUV will be waiting down the street.* I reassured Dallas that if someone found the phone and saw the message, they would just wonder who'd ordered a pizza.

*Are you sure?*

I wasn't sure. I didn't know what obstacles existed inside the garage or if any captors were awake inside the building or even how many there might be. She thought at least three men were there sleeping from the night before, including the gang's kingpin. *People come and go all the time, but it's quiet today and the door is unlocked,* she said. Being early on a Sunday morning after an alcohol- and drug-fueled rager, we agreed there was no better time.

*Delete these messages and hide the phone.*

Britton already had the building pulled up on Google Street View, so I had a visual on the standalone, cinder block warehouse and the industrial buildings surrounding it, but no way of knowing what to expect on the inside. Not even Dallas knew that.

After some convincing, the FBI agent my Homeland Security contact referred me to agreed to park his vehicle down the street, ready to pick up this anonymous woman if she came out alive.

Then it became a waiting game for the signal that Dallas was clear on the inside. It frustrated me to my core that law enforcement couldn't just kick down the door with probable cause and rescue her, but then again, if it was too early for me to be up on a Sunday morning, I imagine securing a warrant from a judge would have been no easy task either. Knowing I could only count on a few hours of goodwill from the FBI before they decided the tip wasn't worth their time, I held my breath hoping Dallas could find her way out.

With the FBI agent standing by after four hours, there was still no word from Dallas.

"Did I give her the wrong instructions?" I vented to Britton. "Did they catch her with the phone? Did the battery die?" I was desperate to know if she was okay, but sending another message would be too risky.

After another hour passed, the FBI agent called to say he would need to disengage if there was no word soon. I couldn't blame him, but every nightmare scenario knocked around inside my head as I pleaded with him to be patient. Nothing would be more dangerous than asking this woman to run and jump off a cliff, I said to him, only to realize that we had packed up the safety net and gone home.

Another hour ticked by. Still nothing from Dallas.

After he'd given me all the time he could, the fed called to say he was standing down. A full rotation had passed with nothing to show for it. "Let me know if she pops up on your radar again. Sometimes, these things end up being a scam," he said.

Not ten minutes later, with the agent still nearby grabbing a bite to eat, her message came—*OK ready*—and the mad scramble began.

I stalled until the FBI agent could reestablish his pickup point two blocks over from the garage, and then I messaged Dallas: *Your Papa C's pizza is ready for pickup! Reply to confirm when you're on your way. We'll keep it hot for you!*

Britton and I sat anxiously at our kitchen table for what seemed an eternity, dinner growing cold, waiting for any sign of what was happening a thousand miles away. Minutes passed like years.

And then it came: *I'm out! In the car!* I held my wife, and we both cried.

I sent Dallas a congratulatory message, struggling to type it with my trembling thumbs.

*Thank you,* she replied. *My real name is Amanda.*

I coordinated with the FBI agent to ensure Amanda was checked into a women's shelter that night.

It was the last time I heard from her.

When most people envision white supremacists, they think of hardened prison thugs, hooded rednecks, tattooed and dead-eyed skinheads, or the now infamous torch-wielding young men at the Charlottesville rally dressed in polos and khakis. While men make up the majority in extremist movements, women like Kassandra and Amanda have also increasingly found a home there.

Because women appear less threatening and represent symbols of purity who can bear future generations of children for the movement, they are primarily used in "traditional" roles or as recruiters and propagandists. Their place in American white supremacy dates back more than 150 years, when the United Daughters of the Confederacy were given the responsibility of installing public monuments across the South to honor men who fought to preserve slavery and to intimidate freed black Americans. Women were also instrumental in publishing educational materials to ensure children in public schools learned a version of history that downplayed the role of slavery in the Civil War and celebrated the Ku Klux Klan, claiming it was "necessary for self-protection against… outrages committed by misguided negroes"—mimicking a statement from the KKK's founding document.

The growing ranks of women, however, have not changed the environment of misogyny and the exploitation of women that is alarmingly common in extremist movements.

Understanding how a lack of empathy might enable violence, it should come as no surprise that many extremist men also practice misogyny. Extremist ideologies are a magnet for men infected with toxic masculinity. Part and parcel is the strict adherence to stereotypical gender roles that limit the kinds of emotions that men are allowed to exhibit.

Most male-dominated societies, which have ruled the earth for millennia, have conditioned its young men not to *feel,* or to suppress their empathy. We've taught boys not to cry, for fear they may appear weak. We routinely shame men for showing emotions or having compassion and instead reinforce the notion of domination through aggression, violence, and war. Throughout generations of men, we've reinforced that progress comes at the expense of others. The results of this practice have manifested in ways that come at a great cost— building walls around vulnerabilities to protect against the unknown, instead of examining failures to repair vulnerabilities.

Acknowledging that a culture of toxic masculinity exists does not suggest all men are "bad" or "evil," or that men are born to be violent conquerors. The concept implies exactly the opposite—that all men *can* be empathetic, loving, and peaceful, if only they can push away the toxins absorbed through centuries of patriarchal culture. And *all* men can take ownership of their actions, good and bad, and grow beyond our fathers' failures.

In many cases involving extremists who are male, the idea that it's okay to be vulnerable, or "human," proves difficult to teach because of how masculinity is twined with misogyny. Believing that men should be in control of the boardroom, the bedroom, and all other spaces in between, some extremist men feel robbed by the progress of women— and minorities—in gaining equal rights. From their skewed perspective, they believe women, having already received unfair advantages in aspects of life that men have traditionally controlled, are taking opportunities that were once sacredly male—in business, politics, and elsewhere. These men confuse what is a frustratingly slow equalization of the sexes in our culture with male oppression.

The need for growth beyond this backward outlook has sharpened as the boundaries of extremist violence widen—extremists have gone from largely marginalizing women from their movements to welcoming them in to their causes to exploit or traffic them like the more traditional criminal element, as the Aryan Brotherhood of Texas did to Amanda, to grooming women as propagandists and zeroing in on them as primary targets of their rage.

As with InCels, a subculture made up mostly of men who claim they are "involuntarily celibate" due to the scorn of women, some extremists have moved on from the simple philosophy of male supremacy to centering women directly in their crosshairs.

Like-minded InCels primarily meet through web message boards on 4chan and Reddit and online multiplayer gaming platforms like Discord. As with most male-dominated extremist movements, InCel forums reveal discussions rooted in misogyny and violence against women. Primary themes include fantasized rape; the murder and subjugation of "unattainable" women, or "Stacys" as they're referred to; violence against other men—"Chads"—who are sexually active; and self-denigration, providing further evidence that outward expressions of "hate" are rooted in self-hatred.

In 2014, a California InCel murdered six people in a stabbing and shooting melee, opening the door to further violence against women by copycats. In his 141-page manifesto, the twenty-two-year-old killer wrote, "I wanted a happy, healthy life of love and sex. But if I am unable to have such a life, then I will have no choice but to exact revenge on the society that denied it to me." In it, he declared war on women.

In April 2018, a Toronto-based twenty-six-year-old praised the California InCel killer in a Facebook message shortly before driving his vehicle into a crowd and killing ten people. His post stated, "The InCel Rebellion has already begun!"

To no one's surprise, significant crossover exists between InCels and supporters of white nationalism and other extremist movements.

When I first saw the headline in my news feed, it sent shivers down my spine. Mention of the Aryan Brotherhood of Texas led me to wonder if Amanda—whom I first knew as *Dallas*—was involved.

*May 1, 2018*—Dallas Observer

*FEDS BUST 51 WHITE SUPREMACISTS FOR DEALING METH AND CHOPPING OFF KIDNAPPING VICTIM'S FINGER*

*Dallas, Texas—Fifty-one individuals are in jail, and six others are being sought after a massive federal investigation into methamphetamine distribution and kidnapping by white supremacist prison gangs in North Texas. According to the Indictment, the defendants are members of, or associated with, various organizations including the Aryan Brotherhood of Texas (ABT). The Indictment further alleges four defendants kidnapped and held a victim for several days to obtain stolen drug proceeds. Defendants pointed a pistol at the victim, hit him with a large wooden object on the back of the head, and used a hatchet to chop off a portion of his index finger. United States Attorney General Jeff Sessions said in a statement: "Not only do white supremacist gangs subscribe to a repugnant, hateful ideology, they also engage in significant organized and violent criminal activity. The quantities of drugs, guns, and money seized in this case are staggering."*

When I learned the dismembered finger in the article didn't belong to a female victim, I felt relieved it wasn't Amanda. Over a year had passed and I hadn't heard anything more from her or the FBI agent once she got to safety. Remembering the tense day of her rescue, I hoped she broke free of her darkness.

# 9

## The Propaganda of Hate

### *Kassandra*

KASSANDRA'S RADICALIZATION AND ITS INTERSECTION with Russian influence makes her story difficult to tell, because for some people "Russian meddling" is "fake news." Her story differs greatly from most other interventions I've experienced—the work was much more time-consuming, hands-on, and research-intensive. While I normally engage in superficial web searches on some of the people I work with to help me better understand the online motivations for their trajectory toward extremism, Kassandra's situation thrust me into intelligence work I hadn't bargained for.

Once the anonymous threats to sever my head started rolling in, I could no longer ignore I was out of my depth. Having never before experienced online attacks of this magnatude, I worried I had ventured out further than I could manage.

While I was in Brussels meeting with an ex-ISIS member, threatening voice messages continued to flood my private line and hundreds of creative death wishes crammed my in-box and social media feeds. Six hours after temporarily taking down my website and the resulting adrenaline hangover had sent me to sleep, the gentle ping of a text message woke me from a dream and yanked me back into a living nightmare I still can't shake.

*You must die.*

More pointed messages lit up my phone screen: *You will endure a slow and painful death. People don't like it when creeps like you stalk little girls.*

*Pedophile Picciolini, you've outdone yourself.*

*Why do you think people need "saving"? What are you saving them from? Kill yourself instead.*

Being on foreign soil made me vulnerable, so I shoved my passport into the front pocket of my jeans and saved my US embassy contact's number in my cell phone. Then, I tried to figure out who to report the threats to. The "little girls" reference confirmed my suspicion the attack resulted from my involvement with Kassandra and Bergsson. Given the breadth of the hacking and harassment campaign, Bergsson had help. Based on what I knew about at least one man behind the alias—Maksim Volkov—the help came from Russian trolls.

But who would believe Russian operatives were manipulating a teenage girl to fool conservative Americans with white-nationalist conspiracy theories? I knew it sounded absurd. But the evidence reminded me it wasn't, so I shared my discovery with a friend who connected me with an old colleague working on Hillary Clinton's campaign staff. I swapped a few emails and some of the data I collected on Bergsson with the staffer before he told me my life was "very interesting" and stopped replying. When I thought about following up again, I realized just how crazy I must have sounded and thought it best not to.

The unbelievable scenario forming in my head made it throb, and I felt a familiar sensation that I hadn't in decades—the same confusion and paranoia that haunted me when I believed that a "race war" was looming. The cacophony of a hundred conversations at the café outside my hotel window and the taxicabs on the Brussels street below blended together in an echo that sounded hollow in my ears. The moist breeze embraced me like a mass of gelatin, and after what seemed like far too long I remembered to breathe. Reality rushed back, leaving behind the taste of fury to burn my throat.

I decided to reach out to another contact at the State Department. She listened carefully and didn't say much.

"You must think I've lost my mind," I finally said.

She claimed she didn't and left it at that. I sensed she was the most patient bureaucrat in the world, and she was humoring me. Turns out she wasn't.

The following day, a State Department security team in Brussels insisted on issuing a protective detail for me, and my transportation for the remainder of my trip was the ambassador's armored Hummer. Still, no one else—not my contact at Homeland Security or the Clinton staffer—had returned my subsequent calls. So, I continued to monitor and archive the Russian troll accounts connected to Bergsson, noting the various pro-Trump and pro-Putin white-nationalist messages they were spreading. I knew I was risking destroying any credibility I had with my government contacts, but I felt I had no other choice. Not only was the safety of a teenage girl and her family at stake, but it was beginning to look like they were pawns in a much larger propaganda scheme to sow discord among Americans during election season.

Perhaps Homeland Security didn't have the power to look into foreign online accounts, but the FBI did. If I could find information on any Americans behind the Bergsson alias, I decided, then maybe I could figure out how to get them to pay attention—and help Kassandra.

While pursuing law enforcement support for Kassandra, I also made it a priority to help her parents assemble the social support she needed, which included a psychologist and a behavioral therapist they were fortunate to have the means to hire. Her twin, Simone, also appreciated the delicate situation and was doing her best to provide her sister with moral support.

I knew Kassandra needed something more, connections beyond her network of family and counselors, to break through her current mind-set. She needed to speak with someone who could contradict the lies she embraced as truth, but who could reach her through an emotional experience instead of debate—she had to *feel* the reality of the hate she was spreading.

A mutual acquaintance introduced me to Elsie, a ninety-two-year-old

American Holocaust survivor who lived in New Jersey, not far from Kassandra's family. Lovely and compassionate, Elsie was eager to meet with Kassandra when I called to ask if she would. She said she always saw the best in everyone, even those who were hell-bent on exhibiting their worst. "I've forgiven even the guards who tortured me and the many other familiar strangers in my barracks at Auschwitz," she told me. Her empathy astounded me.

"What should I say to this girl?" Elsie asked. "How can I change her mind?"

Knowing there was no surefire way to change someone's mind and that every immersion scenario, while different, had the same chance of backfiring, I said, "Tell her how you felt surviving the camps as a young girl, and just be yourself. Let her sit with those emotions. Then leave the rest to her."

I needed to keep the conversation out of Kassandra's headspace and make it something she could experience viscerally.

I picked Elsie up and accompanied her on our first meeting with Kassandra, assuring her I would take over if I felt things were turning disrespectful. She blew a puff of air out of her mouth ostentatiously. "You're so cute, honey," she said, pinching my cheek. "I survived the real Nazis. This poor, confused girl doesn't frighten me. My heart goes out to her."

Kassandra's parents greeted us at the front door and brought us coffee while Elsie and I waited in the kitchen for their daughter to join.

After a few minutes, Kassandra emerged from her room and sat across from us, setting a small folder of notes beside her. Already, I realized the scale of the potential mistake I might have made in bringing Elsie there.

The conversation was congenial at first as they shook hands and made introductions. Then Kassandra opened her folder. While maintaining her composure, she thumbed through the pages, presenting photos and reciting items as "proof" the Holocaust was a massive scam perpetrated by Jews to elicit sympathy and paint Nazis as the "bad guys."

At one point, she claimed the death camp had a swimming pool and marching band.

Elsie let Kassandra talk, and when she finished, she said, "Yes, honey, we dug many holes in the ground. You're right. But they weren't for swimming pools, my dear. They were for burying the dead—men, women, and children, just like you and me. I was your age when I was imprisoned in Auschwitz. We had music—there *was* a band in our camp, so there is some truth in that. Four lovely gentlemen musicians and a woman violinist were made to stand on the train platform and perform when the railcars pulled in carrying people to their deaths. Their serenade was to fool them into thinking they wouldn't be killed on arrival, which was what everyone warned them would happen—and what *did* happen to most. We knew what was going on in other parts of the camp. The band only played their songs when the trains full of frightened people pulled in."

Elsie sipped her coffee. A tear on his cheek, Jack excused himself for the restroom.

"After a while," Elsie said, "there was simply no more music."

She spoke about her life at four brutal concentration camps, including the Nazi medical experiments she endured at seventeen.

"It was only women there," Elsie confided, her voice barely rising above a whisper. "That's how I lost my virginity. I was seventeen—your age—and they took it with a medical instrument."

To let the weight of her story rest on Kassandra, I shifted the direction of our conversation and asked Elsie how she first became imprisoned.

"My father and I were living in Italy," she said, "and Nazi soldiers accused us of signaling enemy airplanes with lit cigarettes. That was a lie. Neither of us smoked, and we wouldn't have known the first thing about signaling planes. Our crime was simply being Jewish."

Kassandra's jaw clenched, her fingers fidgeting with the corners of her papers. While she didn't acknowledge she no longer believed the slaughter of six million Jews hadn't occurred, she agreed there may have been problems with her sources. "I'll look for information to corroborate your story elsewhere," she said, "perhaps at the library, not on the Internet."

It was a small step in the right direction.

After a few visits with Elsie, and what appeared to be a clean break from Bergsson, we all felt Kassandra was doing better, including her therapist. She was more talkative, sharing her feelings, and openly introducing ideas that challenged her old ones for the first time. She seemed contemplative, self-reflective, and focused on her studies—completing the final two credits for her online high school diploma with excellence and talking about college. Her therapist reported that Kassandra was motivated and making progress. She appeared to have fully disengaged from the ideology and was now fixated on her future.

But Kassandra's toxic ICP had not been swapped out for healthier options, and when she became depressed and struggled with her unresolved potholes of alienation and anxiety, she plunged straight back into the world of hate. She re-established contact with Jakob, who was more than eager to lock back on to his unwitting mark. It crushed Jack and Meredith to learn she communicated with him through her e-reader device—the only electronic item they had left in her possession.

I also didn't take Kassandra's backslide well. She had everything going for her—the love of supportive parents, excellent counselors, a sister who championed her, even an inspiring Holocaust survivor as a mentor. She received plenty of support from her family and therapist and ongoing guidance from me. While I've learned to expect some instances of recidivism as a normal part of disengagement work, Kassandra's return to the dark side came with consequences.

The attacks on my website, which I now knew were coming from Bergsson, started again. So, to draw law enforcement into the picture, I doubled my efforts to find proof the alias was tied to American conspirators.

With the help of Google and a YouTube tutorial, I learned to embed an invisible IP tracking code inside of an email, which I then fired off to Bergsson with a Russian subject line daring him to open it: *Приезжайте и поймите меня ублюдок,* or, in plain English, "Come and get me, motherfucker."

To my astonishment, someone opened the email.

When I queried the GPS coordinates of the returned IP, unlike the dozens of bogus IP addresses I collected from his other accounts, this one had been left unprotected. By oversight or human error, someone connected to the Bergsson alias and Kassandra's radicalization—and the massive wave of harassment I was receiving—made the enormous blunder of leaving their computer's IP location discoverable. A major screwup for any hacker or troll worth their salt. A deeper dive showed the hit originated from a location outside of San Francisco, in Union City, California. Google Maps pointed to a small cluster of six possible homes on a residential street.

It was a huge break. This new evidence was what I had hoped for— at least one person who called himself Jakob Bergsson wasn't in Russia but on American soil. I felt nauseous and furious and at the same time hopeful it would help move forward the investigation into who was radicalizing Kassandra and others like her online.

# 10

## The Threats We Ignore

### *Kassandra*

NEARLY A MONTH HAD PASSED since I presented my dossier on Jakob Bergsson to Kassandra and I was still fending off the onslaught of attacks that followed—harassment directed at me and my family: death threats, derogatory memes, the publishing of a dozen slick propaganda videos attempting to defame and discredit me. Though I wanted to fight the attacks, I knew they wouldn't stop until I exposed their source—I needed to pinpoint the California suspect working with the Russian, Maksim Volkov (a.k.a. Jakob Bergsson).

I called an FBI contact I knew in the Chicago Field Office. He and I had worked together in various efforts to counter violent extremism over the years—enough time, I felt, to consider him a colleague and friend. I asked if he could connect me with an agent in Washington, DC, who would meet with me in person.

"It's urgent," I promised, before jumping into a summary of what I uncovered. The propaganda ploys coming from the Bergsson-connected accounts were exploiting alliances forged in previous years between the alt-right and their counterparts in Russia—through people like David Duke and Richard Spencer, who even aligned himself through marriage with a Putin propagandist. The collection of white-nationalist and alt-right accounts I'd tracked were not only pro-Trump and multiplying in quantity before my eyes, they seemed to oddly smack of Russian nationalism, too.

After hearing me out, the agent said he would do his best to help. From his lack of enthusiasm, though, I found him hard to believe. I'd forgotten all about our conversation when the call came a few days later. The lead agent for the FBI's cybercrime unit in DC agreed to meet with me.

The FBI's Washington Field Office looked chiseled from the same giant slab of white granite as the other dozen FBI offices I'd visited around the country. Inside, it had the same cubicle farm chic of an '80s accounting firm.

With less than a week left before the 2016 presidential election, I needed their analysts to see the information I collected on Bergsson as well as the mountain of evidence relating to Russian disinformation peddling. Far from a mob of basement trolls, this concerned national security and hostile foreign actors. The connections I made between an American and players overseas had solidified in the weeks prior, and when I imagined presenting my evidence to the FBI, I pictured the color falling from the agents' faces as their mouths opened in frightened awe before scrambling to throw resources at the threat to neutralize it. Unfortunately, it didn't happen quite that way.

After clearing the security desk, I sat down with Special Agent Danny Howell from the FBI's cybercrime division and walked him through the details of what I found.

But when I said it out loud in person, the words sounded foolish as they escaped my mouth. "I first...I stumbled on this activity because of a specific crime with a young girl...but I also wanted to bring you what I've found that involves Russian intelligence," I said, scattered and stammering. I touched on the physical threat of abduction to Kassandra and Bergsson's multiple aliases, explaining that what I saw had been conducted almost exclusively online. Just when I thought I lost him, he chimed in.

"Like what?" Howell asked, snapping me back into composure.

For the last two months, I told him, I'd been working with a family to help their daughter break away from the white-supremacist movement.

He nodded, squinting. "I thought you said this was about the Internet."

Of course, it had everything to do with the Internet; most extremist activity today takes place online. "The Internet is their new battlefield," I said, "and Russian propaganda efforts are bolstering extremist narratives there." The transnational alliance became more apparent to me after logging messages and accounts tied to my hateful trolling on Twitter and YouTube. But in this room, my recounted theories carried a whiff of paranoia—even for me.

"I have twenty-six gigabytes of data on my laptop," I said, resigning myself to get the information into someone's hands with far more resources than I had at my disposal. I needed to share the evidence I found but I could tell Howell had little time and even less patience for me. With the presidential election less than a week away, it was too late to stop the online influence campaign, even if the FBI dove right in.

My fumbled introduction and the unlikely nature of my tale made it sound like the vision of a maniac. I knew I'd be lucky if anyone so much as opened one file I left behind. "Seriously," I said, "there's a lot of stuff I've saved that you will be very interested to see. Screen grabs, spreadsheets with thousands of account names, videos, and various other assets that link someone in Northern California to a man in Moscow I believe is a Russian FSB asset posing as an American. I've tracked one associate to a location in Union City, Cali—"

Howell interrupted and looked at me as if I just stumbled in from Fourth Street wearing a tinfoil hat. "All right," he said, after taking a loud sip from his coffee mug. "Wait here. I'll get a secure hard drive for you to dump your files to."

I was relieved when he returned with a flash drive, confident I'd gotten through to him.

"But we're a little busy this week," he said. "It's all hands on deck.

They've just tasked my unit with reading through a stack of sensitive government emails that leaked this morning."

"Hillary's stolen emails?" I asked. "I tried warning her, too."

"Can't say." He slurped his coffee again. "Someone will follow up with you if there are questions."

We shook hands and parted ways. Despite following up on multiple occasions, I still haven't heard back from anyone at the FBI about the information I turned over. They had the power to thwart Kassandra's eventual abduction and stop a foreign disinformation machine from rapidly developing into a national security threat and I did all I could do to alert them. I never set out on a mission to uncover and turn over evidence of Russia's complicity with American white supremacists to influence a voting public; my investigation into a young, innocent girl's transformation into a hateful ideologue who advocated for the deaths of Jews, blacks, and immigrants led me there.

I often think about where I went wrong that day. Was it my exhausted appearance or my scattered eagerness that made Special Agent Howell think I was wasting the FBI's time? The wrong agent on the wrong afternoon? Was his team really busy reading Hillary's leaked emails?

For months, I stayed angry. I blamed the FBI for allowing Russia to continue fooling unsuspecting Americans and compromising our election. Then, I blamed myself—someone who, only decades ago, strengthened the same racist ideals that white nationalists and Russian trolls were using to divide us. I had a rare glimpse into their devious strategy but I could not summon the power to stop it.

The more distance I have from the 2016 election, the more I think what might have been flashing across Howell's mind that day was the same kind of dread that shot through me after a white supremacist in Charlottesville killed a peaceful counter-protester. Trump blamed "both sides" for the violence—inducing feelings that started with cold fear in the face of tragedy and ended in outrage that I've warned people of this rise in extremist violence for years. The FBI believed I was paranoid because they had to—because if I was right, and it turned out

I was, the prospect of Russia interfering in our election and the reality of a growing far-right terror threat would be devastating.

Acting from a position of fear and uncertainty is no way for America to confront one of its greatest problems. We cannot shy away from white-supremacist hate and extremism, characterizing it as a fringe problem at the bottom of a long list of national threats because we are intimidated by what we might find when we look in the mirror, or because acknowledging certain types of extremism like white nationalism is politically thorny. If we don't tackle our failures head-on, we will be doomed to repeat them.

After the Trump administration took the White House in 2017, two Department of Homeland Security grants awarded under President Obama's Countering Violent Extremism (CVE) program were revoked. My former nonprofit—the only organization in the United States focused on disengaging white supremacists at the time—was one of two grantees rescinded. They promised us $400,000 to build an online intervention framework for youth at risk of radicalization to extremism. Three weeks after our funds were pulled, the deadly events in Charlottesville occurred.

The Department of Homeland Security (DHS) never fully explained their decision to pull our grant, though speculation abounded—even a personal tweet I made that was critical of Trump and his proposed "Muslim ban" was blamed as the reason for eliminating our funds.* Some former government officials alleged publicly that Katharine Gorka, then a senior official at DHS and a member of President Trump's National Security Council, denied us because she didn't believe white supremacy was a risk to Americans.† Emails later published by the

---

* R. Nixon and E. Sullivan, "Revocation of Grants to Help Fight Hate Under New Scrutiny After Charlottesville," *New York Times,* August 15, 2017, https://www.nytimes.com/2017/08/15/us/politics/right-wing-extremism-charlottesville.html.

† A. Tracy, "'We Are at a Turning Point': Counterterrorism Experts Say Trump Is Inspiring a New Era of Right-Wing Violence," *Vanity Fair,* November 2, 2018, https://www.vanityfair.com/news/2018/11/trump-administration-tree-of-life-shooting-domestic-terrorism.

*Huffington Post* show Gorka also believed anti-racist activists like Antifa represented a greater "actual threat" to the United States than white nationalists did.* They don't—not by a long shot.

In 2017, the FBI reported that since the devastating al-Qaeda terrorist attacks of 9/11, more people have been killed on US soil by white supremacists than by "any other domestic extremist movement."† Why start counting after 9/11, an attack where nearly three thousand people lost their lives because of radical Islamist terrorism and not white supremacy? Political scientists generally argue that 9/11 changed US national security threat perceptions to include global terrorism for the first time, which is why most data sets start in 2001. Plus, if one attempted to document all the carnage inflicted by white supremacists in America prior to 9/11—beginning with Columbus and the colonization by our Founding Fathers—the devastation spanning those centuries would be incalculable. Even if this stain is never wiped clean, we must not allow it to spread.

---

* J. Schulberg, "Trump DHS Official Suggested Antifascists Were 'the Actual Threats,'" *Huffington Post*, April 5, 2019, https://www.huffpost.com/entry/dhs-violent-extremism-katie-gorka-life-after-hate-mpac-antifa_n_5ca787d7e4b0a00f6d3f2e73.

† J. Winter, "FBI and DHS Warned of Growing Threat from White Supremacists Months Ago," *Foreign Policy*, August 14, 2017, https://foreignpolicy.com/2017/08/14/fbi-and-dhs-warned-of-growing-threat-from-white-supremacists-months-ago/.

# 11

## Terror by Another Name

### *Koval*

ADAM KOVAL LOVED GUNS. Big ones. The louder and more powerful, the better. His fascination with firepower began in early childhood. A lonely kid with no close friends, Koval made high-caliber weaponry his passion in life. He imagined the status that came with owning guns, and he fantasized about who he would intimidate and impress once he stockpiled them.

When Koval got bored, he found that some of the best sources online to learn and talk about his gun collection were white-supremacist websites. He became a loyal listener of the Infowars podcast hosted by conspiracy theorist Alex Jones and he read ultraconservative propaganda on Breitbart News—an influential online purveyor of right-wing opinions run then by Trump associate Steve Bannon. Koval developed a taste for identity politics and the unforgiving doctrine of the alt-right and soon found the views on Breitbart weren't extreme enough.

When he looked elsewhere for people who were more interested in action over discussion, it took only a few clicks before Koval was trading Alex Jones and Sandy Hook hoax theories for Adolf Hitler and Holocaust denial. Instead of shunning Koval for his extreme talk, members of the online white-supremacist forums applauded him for his clapback against political correctness. Then, a user on Stormfront took Koval up on his gun talk.

"Just got my fully-auto MAC-10 back from the gunsmith so we can light it up in the desert. Come on out to Death Valley next month. I'll connect you with some comrades who like heavy firepower," wrote the Texas stranger with the screen name Rape.

"Are you serious? Consider it done. I've been reloading ammo all summer," Koval replied through their encrypted chat on the popular online gaming platform Discord. "Got an oil drum full of steel-jacketed .223 rounds buried over at my folks' place outside of Vegas. That little barrel of death plus my AR-15 should hold off the zombie apocalypse until at least 2020."

"They're the best ammunition to stock up on because they're versatile," said Rape. "The government wants to ban them and take your black rifles away—disarm you before the revolution."

"Ain't no zombie revolt gonna scare me," Koval wrote, "and ain't no socialists taking away my weapons either."

"Well, friend, to be fair, zombies are the least of your problems," Rape responded, shifting the conversation. "It's the Zionist Jews and their minions you need to worry about. Bloodsucking kikes are the real poison."

Koval didn't agree with Rape's ultra-extremist views. He didn't know any Jews to speak of or hate them the way Rape did, and Rape's hero worship of Charles Manson and Satan—not to mention his screen name—seemed bizarre. Those things didn't faze Koval too much, though, since he learned from an early age to block negative thoughts out. First, he learned to ignore his father's frequent criticisms—about his weight and a fluttered stride from a bicycle accident at thirteen—then he taught himself to tune out his mother's laments about her unhappiness. But now, Koval's wife was fed up with his regressive spiral into feeling sorry for himself. He couldn't help but get frustrated with her constant encouragement that he needed to get out of the house—to find a hobby and friends. He wanted to keep his wife happy, so that's what he did.

It wasn't long before his new friend Rape recruited him into Atomwaffen Division—the Nazi terror group that even spooks other Nazis.

Appropriating symbols and an old moniker from Hitler's National Socialist Party, Atomwaffen—*atomic weapons* in German—is a well-armed, paramilitary neo-Nazi "death cult" enamored with Satanism and cult leader Charles Manson. They worship the teachings of Adolf Hitler and former American Nazi Party leader George Lincoln Rockwell, which calls for the extermination of Jews, the overthrow of the US government through acts of terrorism, and the assassination of enemies. Members of Atomwaffen Division consider themselves devoutly National Socialist (Nazi), but while most outside observers somewhat mistakenly lump them in with the alt-right and white nationalism writ large, Atomwaffen is altogether a frighteningly different animal. While it's not incorrect to tag a group like Atomwaffen Division with an umbrella term like *white supremacist*—enjoining them with alt-righters, white nationalists, Klansmen, neo-Nazis, white-power skinheads, white identitarians, Christian Identity practitioners, and the like—most white extremists hoping to evade the stigma of militant white supremacy consider Atomwaffen *too* extreme.

Made up of equal parts Hitler's Final Solution, Rockwell's "white power," Manson's helter-skelter vision of igniting revolution, the how-to teachings of James Mason—an American neo-Nazi propagandist who has since the 1980s advocated for "total race war"—and a dash of jihadist-inspired terror, Atomwaffen Division is an extremist group that has created a volatile cocktail of death and destruction seemingly out of obscurity.

Atomwaffen's leaders know how to draw in disillusioned, young white males whose only medium for acceptance and interaction may be the virtual world, and whose shared frustration stems from a real world they perceive has sidelined and emasculated them.

In recent years, they've needed little provocation to unleash their deadly brand of mayhem. Since 2017, young men associated with Atomwaffen Division appear to have committed murder at an alarming rate.

In a horrific anti-Semitic and homophobic killing in January 2018, a twenty-year-old Atomwaffen Division member in California killed a gay, Jewish college classmate, stabbing him over twenty times before burying his body in a shallow grave.*

That same year in May, police charged a twenty-one-year-old member in Florida—the geographic nucleus of Atomwaffen—with possessing functioning bomb-making devices and radioactive isotope materials, which he allegedly intended to use in attacks on synagogues and nuclear power plants. In searching his apartment, police discovered the would-be bomber's eighteen-year-old roommate, an Atomwaffen devotee turned radical ISIS follower, had apparently shot and killed two neo-Nazi friends after they ridiculed his transformation, claiming he'd gone "from Communist to Nazi to full Islamic State"—a prime example of *cult hopping* from one extreme ideology to another to fulfill ICP. Among the suspect's personal possessions, police also found Third Reich paraphernalia, college campus recruitment posters, and a framed photograph of Oklahoma City bomber Timothy McVeigh.

In December 2018, when another seventeen-year-old Atomwaffen supporter in Virginia was rebuked by his girlfriend's parents because they wouldn't allow her to date someone with his extremist beliefs, he allegedly murdered the couple in cold blood.

Members have conducted weapons and combat training in at least four US states in recent years. They have also recruited current and former members of the military, who find their skills valued for leadership roles within Atomwaffen. Drawing on battlefield experience, ex-soldiers have helped shape the group into a loose collection of anonymous terrorist cells. Followers are encouraged to engage in lone wolf–style attacks against people and places that serve minority groups, including the LGBTQ and Jewish communities, government

---

* A. C. Thompson, A. Winston, and J. Hanrahan, "California Murder Suspect Said to Have Trained with Extremist Hate Group," ProPublica, January 26, 2018, https://www.propublica.org/article/california-murder-suspect-atomwaffen-division-extremist-hate-group.

facilities, and such critical public infrastructures as electric power grids, gas pipelines, water filtration systems, and nuclear energy plants. Although it's hard to say how many are part of the group because of their clandestine nature, Atomwaffen claim that one hundred members exist in more than thirty cells across at least twenty-five US states. Even if one hundred operatives seem like a relatively small number for any terror group in a nation as large as the United States, we must not forget it took only nineteen men with two airplanes to murder three thousand people on 9/11. By using digital media and the Internet as a virtual recruiting ground, Atomwaffen Division has reached a significant number of alienated people with their seductive narratives. And while supporters skew younger in age—fifteen to midtwenties—I have communicated with members in their late thirties, who retired from the military with combat skills already in place before finding Atomwaffen.

By early 2018, around the time Koval first contacted me, Atomwaffen cells were already springing up in cities across America. Fortunately for him, he saw through their ruse *just* before it was too late. He reached out to me over email:

> *I was recently outed as a member of a white-power terror group. Figure I've only got two options now. Either make it my life and destroy my family, or get out. I don't know how to do the latter, or if it's even possible at this point. Can you help me? You're my last option.*
> —Adam Koval

I shot back a quick response:

> *Solid assessment. But I see only one option. How can I help?*
> —Christian Picciolini

Koval found his way to me amid a violent life spiral. Undercover journalists caught him bragging in a private online chat about the three-day paramilitary training camp he attended with other Atomwaffen members. He wrote he could be a "weapons armory" for members who needed one and claimed he converted a Czech-made CZ Scorpion rifle to fully automatic. Perfect for a zombie raid—or a race war. He also promised to supply his new comrades with whatever it was they needed for their white revolution.

As Koval fully immersed himself in Atomwaffen Division, he learned the group wanted—as members had announced through YouTube videos and poster campaigns on university and college campuses—to regain things like the "glory of the white race" and "to reign supreme over everything under the burning sun." Pure, unadulterated homegrown hate. That was Atomwaffen's public face, anyway.

At a three-day "Hate Camp" in Death Valley in 2017, organized by Koval's acquaintance Rape, they instead prepared for race war.

Exercises included masked and camouflaged members training with automatic weapons and engaging in hand-to-hand combat techniques. One attendee, a twenty-nine-year-old security contractor from Santa Fe, New Mexico, known only by his alias Totenkopf ("death's head" in German), implemented training sessions that included live-fire drills and belly-crawl exercises. He instructed his fascist stormtroopers how to make homemade thermite grenades for future use on natural gas pipelines. For the grand finale, Totenkopf told his comrades he'd accessed a classified map of the power grid for the entire West Coast of the United States.

Atomwaffen's revolution could now begin.

Totenkopf promised a Hate Camp like none before. And when Totenkopf, who I came to know as Adam Koval, promised something, he delivered.

# 12

## A Withdrawal from Hate

### *Kassandra*

DISENGAGEMENT EFFORTS ARE NEVER EASY—some go sideways or never come full circle, fear takes hold, the complexities of life come into play. Becoming steeped in a mass movement makes leaving and replacing ICP difficult, and when you add a powerful emotion like love to the equation, it can be unpredictable. When I doubt the progress of a person I am working with, I remember my own disengagement and remind myself I can't give up on them—even if efforts appear futile—because they may not believe in themselves. How might my life be different today had people given up on me decades ago? I'm grateful they didn't.

Kassandra's case proved one of the most challenging I've ever experienced—with her feelings for Jakob creating all sorts of thorny obstacles and pitfalls. When I received Meredith's frantic call that Kassandra went missing, I didn't know at the time if it was an abduction or if she had been lured, but I was certain someone behind the Jakob Bergsson alias was involved.

After Jack and Meredith reviewed details of the day with Kassandra's school administrators and campus security, Meredith emailed me video surveillance footage from the dormitory to review after I landed in San Francisco.

A replay of the grainy, closed-circuit imagery showed Kassandra carrying her backpack and violin case and leaving her second-floor dorm room on her fifth day as a college student. The next camera picks her up in the building's first-floor foyer as she exits the stairwell and walks down the main hallway and out the front door. Once outside the building, Kassandra appears to engage in brief banter with the driver of a white, four-door sedan before she gets in the vehicle and they leave. Where she was headed, or which ride-share service—presumably—took her there, was impossible to determine from the angles of the video cameras. I shuddered to think what might have happened to her after they pulled away.

I watched the video again, trying to pick up even the smallest detail, hoping to better understand what happened. A few minutes in, before leaving her room on the second floor, what appears to be a thirtysomething Latino driver exits his white sedan, stands there briefly, and then gets back into the driver's seat of his car. Not enough time or resolution on the camera to get a good enough ID. Three minutes later, Kassandra comes out with her backpack and violin case in tow. If she'd been taken by force, I reasoned, she wouldn't have prepared a backpack or brought her valuable violin along. I watched the video again, and a new detail jumped out: after Kassandra approaches the window of the white sedan and exchanges a few words with the driver, she climbs into the front passenger seat. *Who gets into the front seat of a service car?*

The white car and its license plate are never fully visible on the video, and according to the cell phone Kassandra left behind in her dorm, she hadn't hailed any ride-share or taxi service that day, or ever. She also wiped the call log before ditching her phone. This left us with no clues as to why—or how—a shy and awkward young girl living in a brand-new environment would pick up and disappear.

Kassandra had sent Meredith a text message the night before when Meredith was already asleep. *I'm sorry, mom,* was all it said. The only other item of substance was an unsent follow-up text to her mother reading: *Goodbye.* It made me think she'd gone willingly, even if she was unsure of who would be meeting her on the other end. It was clear to all of us, though, after twenty-four hours passed with no word, it wasn't home Kassandra was headed for.

*It's okay, sweetie. I love you. Anything fun planned for today?* Meredith typed back early the next morning. She assumed Kassandra was being remorseful about the weapons-grade tantrum she threw the week before leaving for school. It was one of many in recent months, though Meredith felt the text apology was a positive sign—given the divot Kassandra left in the wall with the mug she'd thrown from across the room in a fit.

Meredith was anxious about Kassandra going off to college so soon after they weaned her off Bergsson. Even the thought that her daughter would be on her own, among strangers—a stark contrast from huddling in her room on her computer for years—took a toll. Kassandra's therapist encouraged her independence, so Meredith and Jack agreed with their daughter's wish to enroll in a small, private college in rural, northern New Jersey. A supportive attitude from school administrators about the family's request for extra security measures for Kassandra provided Jack and Meredith with some comfort, but they remained cautious.

In the month leading up to Kassandra going away to college, it appeared she disengaged from her white-nationalist ideology. She stayed off the Internet and stopped discussing her views obsessively, filling the extra time practicing violin. I understood why Jack and Meredith felt they needed to restrict Kassandra's Internet access at the time—we knew Bergsson was a dangerous fraud and Kassandra was still resisting her parents' attempts to stop contacting him—but I worried about their approach. As reticent and disconnected as Kassandra was, it also stripped her of any opportunity to find positive outlets for ICP. A more monitored approach with a solid plan to help build her resilience and with clear expectations was my suggested route forward. For extremists whose ideological mission statement is based on the notion of protecting something of "great value" from being lost, taking things away from them and hoping they'll change views on their own rarely works. We were all proud of Kassandra for staying "clean" of both hate and Bergsson, but we were very afraid of a relapse, too.

Knowing a long road to recovery was still ahead for Kassandra, Jack and Meredith were relieved to have at least temporarily averted a catastrophe of losing their daughter to a hideous ideology—and maybe the lure of a sexual predator who'd since gone dark. The future looked brighter for their daughter, and they were eager to welcome her back to "normal."

As the start of college neared, Kassandra sounded more content and grounded to her therapist, but she still hadn't discovered a healthier sense of self, connection, or meaningfulness to replace what she gave up in the movement and Bergsson. Kassandra turned eighteen two weeks before going off to school on her own, and her attitude, despite some lingering bouts of spontaneous rage, became more tolerable to her parents. I cautioned Jack and Meredith that a sudden transition from her solitary white-nationalist bubble to the sensory overload of a college campus so soon might be too much for Kassandra. While I was excited she made it through her final semester of online high school, experienced an uneventful summer break, and tested above average into a private college where she could make real friends and live in the real world, I was concerned with how vulnerable and impressionable Kassandra would be, far from her family and without a healthy community to fall back on when she needed it—and she *would* need it.

Kassandra's desire to live on her own in a relatively diverse environment full of people and ideas that had been outside her comfort zone her entire life worried all of us. But those were Kassandra's wishes, and she wanted to prove she could do it, to her family and to herself. Knowing it wouldn't be easy for the identical twins to be apart, Simone provided tremendous support for her sister in daily phone calls and texts after she herself went away to school in Rhode Island, another drastic change Kassandra would need to grow accustomed to. Jack made Kassandra's school aware of her sensitive situation, and Meredith devised a plan for easy access to the resources she would need there to thrive—a school counselor, a behavioral therapist near campus, and an emergency list of local law enforcement contacts should an emergency arise. All any of us could do, we thought, was actively support Kassandra's recovery.

I hoped that by building up Kassandra's confidence and setting her off on an intellectual awakening, college social life would help her fill the voids left by the separation from Simone and her former sense of ICP, and that it might introduce her to new groups where she could flourish and feel supported. But it didn't; Kassandra was not yet properly equipped to be on her own.

With Jack and Meredith in direct contact with college security and now with local police about their missing daughter, I knew that pinning down more details on the Bergsson identity was the only way to help find her. Unless Kassandra was still in the immediate area of her school, which I doubted, local cops wouldn't be of much help. The FBI had also made it clear to me—though not in so many words—I was on my own.

After landing in San Francisco and settling into my hotel room just outside of Union City, I reviewed my notes on Bergsson and returned to the Google Street View images of the small grouping of six homes, one of which housed Bergsson's unprotected IP address. As I looked closer, I noticed what I hadn't paid much attention to before: parked in one of the driveways was what appeared to be a white Mercedes sedan.

There was, I recalled, a white Mercedes in an old photo that Jakob had emailed Kassandra. The Russian man I linked to Bergsson, Maksim Volkov, also fancied that brand of luxury car on his VK page. I pulled up Bergsson's images from my hard drive and confirmed the car fetish. The white vehicle shown picking up Kassandra on surveillance video could also have been a Mercedes, but the footage was unclear, so I couldn't be sure. Unable to confirm the make of the car on video, I chalked it up to coincidence.

Frustrated at finding no smoking gun and desperate for anything to help Kassandra, I decided to drive into Union City and scope out the block of houses for myself.

I urged Jack and Meredith to stay back in New Jersey to work with the local resources instead of joining me across the country in California. I was operating on intuition I wasn't certain would prove fruitful—it was better for them to stay close to home in case Kassandra decided to return for some reason. There was still hope of her coming back on her own, given we didn't know if Kassandra had been abducted or if she'd gone willingly. As a precaution, Jack alerted the New Jersey State Police, who added Kassandra to the National Missing and Unidentified Persons System to widen the net.

For two days I sat in my rental Jeep eating pizza out of cardboard boxes, watching the six homes I identified, looking for a white Mercedes and anyone entering or leaving the addresses of interest. It proved underwhelming to say the least—being a lifelong Chicagoan, I found it hard to like California-style pizza. And with very few interesting people coming or going, time passed slowly.

I needed a pretense for whoever lived in these homes to poke their heads out so I could see them up close. I decided to order a pizza and attempt to hand-deliver it to each of the six addresses so I could peek inside. I'd check out whoever answered, maybe ask a friendly question, and as they got suspicious—which was inevitable—I could explain I had the wrong delivery address and move to the next house on my list. I hoped to recognize somebody—anyone from the handful of people I suspected were linked to Bergsson—maybe elicit a surprise reaction if someone recognized me from their incessant trolling. Hell, if nothing else, it was my dinner—even if it wasn't Chicago-style deep dish.

I picked up my phone and hit redial to order a large pepperoni pizza. "The name for the order is Jakob Bergsson," I said. "I'll be there in thirty minutes to pick it up."

I rang the doorbell of the first house just after ten that evening. When no one came to the door, I rang again. Still, no answer. As I turned toward the sidewalk for the next home, the porch light came on behind me, and a woman called out from behind a screened window.

"Hello, can I help you?"

"Hi, I have a pizza delivery...for, uh, I think it says Jakob. I can't quite read the last name or the last two numbers of the street address, so I apologize if I guessed wrong. I keep reminding them to replace the printer ribbon at the shop."

"Pizza? *Ahora?* I don't think Santiago's home right now. It's late, but let me see if he's here. One minute. Let me check."

"No need, ma'am, the ticket looks like it says it's for Jakob, not Santiago."

I had the wrong house.

"Oh, he goes by Jake. He hates when people call him Santiago. One moment."

Her words cut through my eardrums like knives. *Bingo.*

The woman disappeared, returning to the open window a minute later. "Not home," she said, shaking her head. "He's away camping with friends. You've got the wrong house, sir."

I apologized for my mistake and made my way to the street, trying to contain my excitement about hitting a massive breakthrough.

Through sheer luck, the first address on my list ended up being the place I searched night and day for over a year to find. My hunch that whoever picked up Kassandra would drive to Union City—the IP location I pinpointed for the FBI nine months earlier, inclusive of the Russian troll campaign—had panned out. With any luck, Jakob would show up soon—and Kassandra would be with him.

# PART TWO

# RADICAL

## "The True Believer"

*It is the True Believer's ability to "shut his eyes and stop his ears" to facts that do not deserve to be either seen or heard which is the source of his unequaled fortitude and constancy. He cannot be frightened by danger nor disheartened by obstacle, not baffled by contradictions, because he denies their existence.*

—Eric Hoffer, *The True Believer*

*We must secure the existence of our people and a future for white children.*

—David Lane, The Fourteen Words

# 13

## Lone Wolf

### *Dylann*

HE COULD HAVE CRASHED AT THEIR TRAILER AGAIN. His friend's mom would have let him—just like the other times he needed somewhere to go after fighting with his dad. But Dylann decided to sweat it out and sleep in his car instead. Even though he detested sweating, it might be his last chance to be alone before hitting the road. Listening to classical music, of all things, calmed his anxieties and frequent delusions, and he could enjoy it in his car for as long and as loud as he wanted without anyone calling him a "faggot" or "pussy."

Preparation for Dylann's road trip took weeks—stocking up on supplies, scouting historic locations, and making checklists of old classmates and churches. The money his dad gave him for his twenty-first birthday was enough to buy the handgun he wanted, but ammunition for it was expensive. He'd become obsessed with online videos of hollow-points punching holes the size of golf balls in ripe Georgia watermelons, so he worked odd jobs until he could afford to fill his magazines with the same rounds.

He prayed the cartridges he snapped into place would find their targets and honor his führer. With his angels of death in final formation, Dylann packed up the last of his gear and set off on his solitary, two-hour drive to Charleston.

At 8:15 p.m. on June 17, 2015, within hours of publishing a detailed online manifesto to outline his motives, Dylann Roof arrived at the Emanuel African Methodist Episcopal (AME) Church in Charleston, South Carolina. He parked his black Hyundai Elantra in a spot next to the building, shut the ignition off, and closed his eyes. He unscrewed a bottle of booze and lifted it to his lips. After taking three long, deliberate swigs in perfect succession and sucking in three quick breaths to calm his nerves followed by three repetitive touches of the door handle, he was ready to save the white race from extinction.

Dylann wore a wrinkled, gray sweatshirt, black chinos, and tan construction boots. He carried a loaded .45-caliber Glock tucked inside his waistband. Steadying himself after exiting his car, he adjusted his belt before entering the historic church through its unlocked door. In the basement of the warmly named Mother Emanuel—the first independent black church in the United States, founded in 1816— he encountered twelve black congregants gathered in prayer and Bible study.

Even before he entered, Mother Emanuel's history was long and complicated. Natural disasters had leveled the building twice. The Confederacy banned its existence and shuttered it along with other prominent black churches in the South until whites burned it to the ground as retribution for a slave revolt. Charleston's black community came together to rebuild her, and each time she rose from the dead. Emanuel AME would survive to become the cornerstone for black Charleston and American civil rights when Booker T. Washington and Dr. Martin Luther King Jr. delivered messages of hope and resistance to generations of Americans from her pulpit.

Mother Emanuel's loving arms welcomed everyone.

The small group of faithful worshippers gathered for prayer that evening was a tight-knit group of friends and family. Without hesitation, eight women, a promising young man, an elderly minister, and a tender-aged girl, along with their beloved leader—an admired South Carolina state senator—welcomed the unfamiliar white man as he entered their Lord's home.

"Would you like to join us in praise, young man?" asked the preacher.

Dylann lowered himself down onto a metal folding chair in the back of the room, his gun resting heavy and cold against his sweaty back. Distracted by the scent of old incense and the group's noisy recital of prayer, he thought of how he'd have to polish the pistol soon or it might rust. He sat silently for forty-five minutes with the black strangers and observed their prayer.

"I shouldn't do this," Roof said out loud as he rose from his chair, according to accounts of those in the room with him. "They're nice," he rationalized again to no one in particular.

But Dylann believed their black skin meant they were evil—an inferior "mud race" who were raping and spilling the blood of innocent whites at an unholy rate. To secure the existence of future white generations, he was convinced he must eliminate them.

Even if the parishioners were kind to Dylann and treated him with respect, it could not erase all the violence blacks were committing against whites; violence that was more significant and destructive, he thought, than what these twelve souls trembling before him would endure. He believed he was a messenger, answering the call to show other whites how to stand up and save themselves while there was still time. Only this moment mattered to Dylann. The future of the white race rested on his ability to follow through, and that meant more to him than anything else in his life ever had.

He couldn't contain his anxiety any longer. As reams of fabricated and fraudulent black-on-white crime data circulated through his subconscious, Dylann rose from his chair in the prayer circle and reached for the semiautomatic weapon in his waistband. Devoid of human emotion, he raised his arm, aimed, and squeezed the trigger—repeatedly. While his innocent victims cried and held each other, shutting their eyes in urgent pleas to their Creator, he shot each of them at least five times.

Standing over one of the distraught survivors, her dying son bleeding out next to her on the church floor, Dylann said, "I'm going to leave you here to tell the story."

Then, he turned the gun on himself. *Click!* It was empty. *Heil Hitler,* he thought.

He slid the hot steel back into his waistband and climbed the stairs of the church basement and exited the building. He calmly got into his car and drove away—leaving behind nine departed souls and only three of Mother Emanuel's children to survive the hellfire and tell his wicked tale.

Four months before his deadly attack on parishioners at Emanuel AME, Dylann Roof published an anonymous Craigslist ad for someone to join him on his road trip to Charleston. In it, he wrote he would accept any traveling companions except for "Jews, queers, or niggers." He followed the racist stipulation with perhaps his only honest revelation: "I am in bed, so depressed I cannot get out of bed. My life is wasted. I have no friends even though I am cool. I am going back to sleep." These words, which echoed Roof's troubled childhood, revealed the depth of isolation that led to his radicalization.

Dylann didn't own a cell phone, but shortly before the murders, he used a computer at the public library to register a Facebook page. There, as if creating a hit list, Dylann reconnected with old classmates—most of them black.

On his Facebook page, Roof uploaded photographs of himself sitting on a wrought iron chair gripping a gun in one hand and a Confederate flag in the other. Aviator glasses hanging down on his nose, he cocked his head forward to reveal the tips of his iceberg-cold eyes. He posed for pictures at Confederate monuments, bragging on social media that South Carolina was once the largest slave-owning state. He gloated about his great-great-grandfather who had bought a nine-year-old black girl after he retired from the Confederate army.

His pictures reminded me of a photo I took at seventeen, when I'd posed at the gates of the Dachau concentration camp in Germany, giving a Nazi salute. I considered—not for the first time—the damage that photos like that could cause, fear visible in the stern glare of a stranger gaping at my obscene pose—and the path I almost kept on out of fear of reprisal, as Roof had chosen.

By this point, Dylann's obsessive preoccupation with (or paranoia about) racial purity had launched him on a meticulous search of his online ancestry records, through which he sought to reassure himself he had no "mixed-race" blood flowing through his veins. In line with what racist conspiracy theory far-right propagandists call the "Great Replacement," he believed white men ruled America but that whites were being outbred and displaced by "inferior" races through low white birthrates, abortions, crime, and race-mixing.

On his fateful drive to Charleston, Dylann stopped at the beach. In the wet sand on the shore of Sullivan's Island, where tens of thousands of West African captives disembarked ships and became slaves, he traced the numbers *1488,* combining the code for *Heil Hitler* ("88") and the white-supremacist "Fourteen Words" mantra coined by an imprisoned white supremacist in 1985: *We must secure the existence of our people and a future for white children.* Alongside the traced number, Dylann drew an Odal rune, an ancient Viking symbol honoring the Norse god Odin, which white supremacists have co-opted from practicing pagans to represent white power.

It took years for Dylann to escalate to this point. The beginnings of his gradual descent into violent racism were somewhat typical—with his parents' divorce uprooting him from community and setting him off on a precarious search for his ICP. After leaving the home his parents built together, Dylann attended seven different schools during the nine years his father and stepmother continually relocated for work. Any search for playground friends and a community to call one's own would have been trying under those circumstances. For Dylann, whose pursuits may have also been exacerbated by mental health issues, it was especially difficult.

While it's unknown which condition—or conditions—Dylann Roof suffers from, in part due to his adamancy during his murder trial to have his own mental health records suppressed, his history of behavioral activity (police had interacted with him during a minor prescription drug offense) and his admitted drug and alcohol consumption have led psychologists to believe he battles clinical depression, a mixed-substance-abuse disorder, and multiple mental health disorders, including autism spectrum disorder (ASD). The disorders alone didn't make him a killer—no specific mental condition can cause someone to become a white supremacist or embrace violence—but left untreated, stigmatization of Dylann's conditions and marginalization could have contributed to the alienation that developed his anger and drove him toward hatred, including ideations of revenge and murder.

Though I don't believe anyone is born a hater, hate was certainly no stranger to Dylann. He'd become exposed to racism at an early age in Columbia, South Carolina, where it wasn't rare to witness bigotry firsthand.

When his parents divorced in 2007 after ten years of a rocky marriage, Dylann's relationship with them—the only real connections he shared in life—disintegrated. He began drinking heavily and abusing prescription pills to both stir and settle his anxiety. When he wasn't feeling depressed, the volatility of his unexpected moods thrilled him until he crashed into depression. As his mental health deteriorated, Dylann's isolation also intensified.

He grew lonelier and more isolated, unable to connect with other students as he shifted around between different schools and began looking for scapegoats for his frustrations. He started spending more time alone, reading about politics and "alternative" news on the Internet. Raised in a region of America that continues to reckon with its history of slavery and a long legacy of racism, Dylann latched on to what might have been the most convenient target for his rage: African Americans.

Believing his life was "irredeemably soiled" by what he thought were inferior races of people, Dylann felt there was no hope for personal advancement or satisfaction. Reaching the level of a *true believer*—a "martyr" willing to sacrifice their life or the lives of others for a cause—Dylann Roof sought self-renunciation from a world he viewed as rotten, and tried to correct it through violence.

Dylann Roof's descent points to how effective extremists have become in furthering their hateful causes online. His radicalization brought to light a new, alarming frontier: young white men finding extremism not through any single individual recruiter but through extremist narratives floating around in cyberspace. With social media and web discussion boards, the Internet has become the primary hub of most extremist interaction, recruitment, and plotting. As extremists learn to wield its power, many have moved from targeting teens for recruitment in alleys (such as my onetime recruiter did to me) and public spaces to targeting new recruits online.

In just seven months, Dylann went from a lost teenager—albeit one with racist inclinations—searching for ICP to a violent extremist. No one in the white-power movement sought him out; he wasn't invited to attend a skinhead concert or a Klan rally, and he hadn't been coaxed to attend any meetings. In fact, he never met another white-supremacist extremist in person. The culture of violent extremism—the racist ideology that taught him to blame his failures on others, and an online community of like-minded people—became so intoxicating to Dylann, it pulled him in without anyone's effort but his own.

He became a follower of groups like the Council of Conservative Citizens (CCC), who he felt weren't afraid to "rip the hijab" off liberal "political correctness" and report on what was important. Jews and nonwhites were to blame, he believed, for the creeping death of white European culture, and the survival of his race was dependent on eradicating them. The CCC's home page, packed with headlines and links to detailed bogus reports about "antiwhite" crimes in the United States, told him so. Perhaps, if the more benign-sounding *CCC*—formerly known by the more accurately named White Citizens' Councils and now designated as a hate group by the Southern Poverty Law Center—thought to replace the three *C*s with *K*s, Dylann could have spotted their dubious agenda. But its racist rebranding was successful, and the dangerous mistruths the organization published on its website convinced Dylann that black "thugs" were responsible for waves of unreported rapes against white women—and numbers were trending up fast.

The fraudulent black-on-white crime statistics that Dylann pored over seemed undeniable proof that hordes of violent black people were, in his words, "taking over and destroying our country." He was wrong, as was all the information he ingested—and kept ingesting—online, and he based his fateful decision to kill on that fake and dangerous misinformation. Dylann fell so deep and fast into a fake news rabbit hole it consumed him.

In the months leading up to the attack, Dylann posted venomous diatribes and rantings online. Sometimes, the posts were rancorous and openly racist. Other times, his hate wore away just enough to reveal a disturbed young man with a capacity for intellect. More than just screeds and hateful opinions, Dylann left behind clues in his writings about his motivation to kill.

Dylann Roof's headfirst swan dive into the swamp of white nationalism began after reading movement propaganda and conspiracy theories on websites like Reddit and 4chan. Referrals from those platforms led him to other fringe networks, and he found his confidence (an aspect of his broken ICP search) on a website called Stormfront—a white-supremacist forum with a cult following that includes almost every racist mass murderer of the last two decades. There, he immersed himself in racist theories based on manipulated crime data, reading articles about events and characters that were completely fabricated.

White-power propaganda music was also an influence on Roof. In one of his first postings on the Stormfront forum in February 2015—four short months before his deadly attack in Charleston—he asked for the racist community's help in identifying music he heard in an HBO documentary about skinheads.

Using the screen name LilAryan, Roof wrote:

*I was wondering if you knew the name of the band. [The song] went:*

*Skinheads have the upper hand,*
*White man's strength will save our land.*
*Stand together. Unity is key.*
*Niggers back to Africa, AmeriKKKa for me.*

As his earliest online posts revealed, Dylann was radicalized just seven months prior to his murderous attack, and solely by the online misinformation he devoured—fake news, conspiracy theories, and falsified crime data published by the CCC and other far-right websites. Creeping through the minefield of his mental health and his parents' divorce, while absorbing the bigoted, damaged environment that was his home and geography, he found comfort in bad research that played into his anxieties. Blacks were killing whites in record numbers, his findings suggested, another "fact" he believed the "Jew-owned" mainstream media was covering up—just like the message boards told him.

Two years after the attack inside Mother Emanuel, a journalist interviewed me about hate music on the Internet and the influence it had on Dylann Roof's radicalization. We were in my home in Chicago, and the anchor pointed me to a Stormfront post Roof made about a band whose lyrics he quoted. The reporter asked me what I thought it meant.

She didn't know it when she asked—and I certainly wasn't aware beforehand—but as I studied the song, there was a reason its lyrics felt familiar. The words Dylann Roof had quoted were mine. It was a song I'd written and recorded with my white-power band twenty-five years prior.

My words called for violence against blacks and Jews, a directive I knew then would encourage violence. Despite years of online takedown reporting and letters sent to overseas record labels that own the rights to my old music, my old band's "hate rock" propaganda that polluted the world during my youth was online and influencing a new generation of violence decades later. The realization that the words I once vomited out in ignorance would live on for an eternity crushed me.

Sometimes I wake up in the middle of the night or think I've woken, and often there are faces that come to me. The lineup contains nine people whom I've never met. They're praying together, hands clutched, gathered as a family, and—not because I deserve their welcome, which I fear I don't—they wave for me to join them at a dinner table. Across from me in the circle sits a scowling young, white man with his head down, whispering and glancing up at me occasionally, a pistol resting in front of him.

As he reaches for the gun, I jump. I recognize it—it's the one I carried as a young skinhead, but now it's his. Then I hear my old song, the one Dylann Roof posted, and I'm hurled backward. Each time I have the dream, it's more unpleasant—time moves faster and it gets harder to speak. I can't remember what I want to say to the young man across from me when he raises his head or what I need to say to him before he grabs the gun. Time runs out as my words form, and then I wake in a cold sweat.

The words always come out too late. I want to tell everyone to run from the young man, and I beg for my gun back.

# PART THREE

# DE-RADICALIZATION

## "The Enlightened Seeker"

*The reality of the other person is not in what he reveals to you, but in what he cannot reveal to you. Therefore, if you would understand him, listen not to what he says but rather what he does not say.*

—Kahlil Gibran, *Sand and Foam*

*He who is devoid of the power to forgive is devoid of the power to love. There is some good in the worst of us, and some evil in the best of us. When we discover this, we are less prone to hate our enemies.*

—Dr. Martin Luther King Jr.

# 14

## The Seven "L" Steps of Disengagement

D R. MARTIN LUTHER KING JR. taught us, "Darkness cannot drive out darkness; only light can do that. Hate cannot drive out hate; only love can do that." Despite the overwhelming hatred Dr. King experienced during his lifetime—and since his assassination in 1968 at the hands of a white supremacist—he has emerged as one of our greatest and most revered Americans.

My disengagement framework is rooted in Dr. King's profound theory of radical empathy. Structured into what I call the "Seven 'L' Steps of Disengagement": *Link, Listen, Learn, Leverage, Lift, Love,* and *Live;* my theory is built on the idea that no person is born to hate—it is a learned behavior. And if it's learned, it can also be unlearned through empathy.

I honestly don't know if everyone can be "saved" from the clutches of hate and extremism; I simply don't have that answer. But I do know we must be able to peer through our human ugliness into our brokenness to ever find out. In my experience, I have found that most extremists want to break free of their hateful or violent lives—if given the chance.

It's a difficult concept to grasp—to embrace the haters—but if we hope to transcend the racists who judge and hurt the people they've never met, we must at least attempt to interpret *why* they hate, so we can prevent it from taking hold of future generations.

Establishing a *link* with an extremist does not mean coddling or appeasing their detestable views or meeting hate halfway. It does not grant them permission to spew bile, nor should it enable further abuse. Instead, empathy pierces the armor of hate to provide a glimpse beneath the rancor of belief to the fractured individual hiding behind it.

Before unwinding the wrong turns they've made in pursuit of hate, identifying which potholes propelled them there is key, and that's usually where I come in. I've stood in their boots, so I can relate to the trauma—it *is* traumatic—stemming from their toxic ICP. I avoid dismissing them and I don't use shame or engage them in debate. Arguing never works; it pushes them away, further isolating and entrenching them in harmful and potentially dangerous ways. Instead, I draw them closer by asking about their personal stories, then I *listen* for potholes.

The key to impactful listening is not sympathizing in ways people might want us to. Great listeners don't just hear the words people say, they listen to *learn* the ambitions behind them. Developing a strong understanding of what motivates someone to hate is critical, since emotional obstacles—not logic or even the ideologies used to justify violence—are the underpinnings of extremist behavior. Ideology is but the final component locking into place that grants license to lash out in a certain direction.

Over time, with space for self-reflection, hatred for others often reveals itself as the projection of gaping deficits of love or respect for oneself. It amazes me every time I see the crutches of hate jettisoned and watch prejudice melt away, all without aggressively confronting someone about their nasty beliefs. It's why I despise the phrase *Once a Nazi, always a Nazi*. Not only can I personally attest the statement is false, limiting someone's ability to *leverage* opportunities for growth is counterproductive to preventing hate. It mirrors and emboldens it.

Instead, enlisting partners to help an individual build resilience and restore their self-confidence establishes a strong foundation for ongoing positive change. Genuine transformation takes not just a village but a very patient one. Guidance and access to ongoing aftercare are vital.

Once pothole repair is under way, a reliable road map that fosters the ICP necessary for resilience can help *lift* the individual to a space where they can learn to *love*—through immersive experiences that challenge their previously held notions. Only then can they learn to truly *live* a happy, meaningful, and productive life on their own terms again—or for the first time.

The key to lasting success—and I believe this to be the most important factor in determining full and genuine disengagement—is committing to live a happy, meaningful, and productive life by repairing the harm caused along the way.

This compassionate approach to confronting extremism is the only method I have seen succeed in breaking hate. As Dr. King said, *"Hate cannot drive out hate; only love can do that."*

# 15

## See the Child, Not the Monster

### Step One: Link
### *Koval*

*Establishing a link requires building rapport and trust through nonconfrontational and meaningful interactions that challenge existing narratives—but that do not directly address ideology—and foster an environment free from fear of judgment, emotional repercussion, or shame. Building this bridge first is of utmost importance, even if progress appears implausible or negligible at first. Force yourself to see an imperfect human being instead of the hateful persona they want you to see.*

BY DAYBREAK, THE LAS VEGAS STRIP was already sizzling at a dangerous 108 degrees. The dry desert air hit me like a blast furnace when I stepped out of the taxi. I chose the Tropicana to meet with Adam Koval, both because I thought it might be easier to blend in there versus a place like Caesars, and I found it oddly compelling that an ex-terrorist and a current Atomwaffen terrorist were secretly meeting at an old-school Rat Pack casino. I wasn't sure about Koval, but I was all in for this high-stakes crapshoot.

I had no idea who to look for. Koval and I had never met, though we exchanged enough emails for me to become intrigued by his story. His initial message to me sounded dire. ProPublica, the news organization that leaked his private messages from the encrypted platform where he communicated with other Atomwaffen members, had outed him as an organizer of the Hate Camp in Death Valley, and Koval didn't know what to do about the exposure. I assured him reaching out to me was a good first step but that he needed to extricate himself from Atomwaffen Division and the extremists he was involved with immediately. After his identity went public, FBI agents questioned him. The feds were interested in details about the classified power grid map he claimed he could get his hands on, but it turned out the anonymous Atomwaffen member who promised it to him never delivered. They released Koval and cleared him for lack of evidence.

Being publicly exposed made Koval anxious and paranoid—his extremist life had been a secret one. His wife tolerated his obsession with firepower, but she never suspected his fanaticism involved a white-supremacist terror group. Understandably, she was furious and felt betrayed when the news came out. She threatened to leave him and it sent Koval into a panic. She was his rock, he told me, and the only good thing that ever happened to him. Koval loved her and couldn't imagine his life without her.

His anxiety stemmed from the stress of keeping his secret and mitigating the constant worry with heavy prescription painkillers. Options for escaping the predicament unscathed dwindled with each passing minute and the consequences of his double life grew grimmer by the hour.

He swallowed a palmful of pills and pulled back the living room curtain to see if the journalists had left—or if any Atomwaffen mates developed a taste for revenge. That's when Koval decided he'd done enough damage. He reached out to me the next day for advice on what to do.

After reviewing everything I learned about Koval from our emails of the previous week, I scanned my hotel room for any potential risks the space posed. It felt reckless meeting Koval for the first time in such a private place. I worried about an ambush, so I walked the area outside my room to check for vulnerabilities, just in case.

Unlike most other visitors to Sin City, I actually preferred more visibility to privacy and a way to escape should I need one. Emergency exit stairwells bookended the long hallway outside my room. The open rooftop fifty feet below my window meant that particular escape route was a one-way swan dive to the Clark County meat locker, even if I could get the window open—they keep them sealed in Vegas to stop jumpers. The bathroom door locked but its hollow cardboard core would offer little resistance if things went haywire. Less than ideal, the room would have to do. The unfortunate coincidence of a bow hunting convention in town meant none of the rooms on lower floors were available. I was eight stories up, on a tightrope, and alone.

Koval needed a safe way out, and it was clear how worried about his safety he was. If I was reckless in setting up the meeting so soon after he reached out, it was because I knew he was at a crossroads facing what was probably the most critical decision of his life. I couldn't let too much time pass, even if Koval was affiliated with a dangerous terrorist group.

If there's one thing I learned along my own journey, it's that having empathy and offering compassion—often for those we feel least deserve it—*is* the only path toward change. Hold people accountable for their actions, question things, speak truth to power, get mad as hell, and prepare to fight back if attacked, but drill down to the underlying motivations that led them there. Having lived on both sides of hate, I see it in ways that are difficult for most to understand. Strangers, people I believed I hated on principle alone, showed me empathy when I least deserved it. It was a triumph of humanization over demonization. Now I use the same tactic—to *see the child, not the monster* in people. This mantra is the foundation on which I build the trust necessary to help people disengage from extremism, and it gives me important perspective to suss out fear and rationalizations from core values.

When I called Koval the night before to confirm our meeting plans, he spoke breathlessly, sounding scared, desperate. He knew few people would be willing to help someone like him—I also understood why others might be reluctant—and I might be the only person left willing to hear him out. I made sure he knew that if he could prove to me he was genuine about disengaging, I would keep my promise to help him.

"I once needed someone to believe in me and help me move forward," I confessed to Koval. "I know it feels daunting to walk away and start your life over, but I promise you can do it—and it's worth it. There are other folks like me who found their way out and are now doing amazing things with their lives."

With those few words of hope, I established a bond of trust with Koval. Now, preparing to meet him in person for the first time, I stuffed away any last-minute regrets.

My heart skipped when I heard the timid knock on my hotel room door.

I greeted Koval, and he extended his hand across the threshold to meet mine. He was taller than I expected, with a high forehead and an auburn beard that was even longer than the fiery unkempt locks on his head. His eyebrows ended shy of the bridge of his nose, which looked jagged, like it bounced punches more than a few times. I wondered if it was due to an adolescence full of roughhousing, or if bullies had picked on him when he was a kid for being born that way.

I gestured for Koval to enter and take a seat near the desk at the far end of my suite. Without turning his back to me, he slid past me in the doorway, walking with a limp, and sank into an armchair instead. He shifted nervously in his seat as he watched me approach.

Koval didn't look like a stereotypical white supremacist from my day, with no identifiable tattoos and the tangled hair of a 1980s rock god. He wore a crisp, crimson T-shirt with SINNERS SPORTSMAN'S CLUB printed across the chest in thick, white script. I smelled the cloying scent of tobacco on him. Having abstained from cigarettes for over a year by then, my sudden craving made it hard to focus. I reminded myself it was not the time to battle my own demons.

I took a swig from the heavy glass bottle of mineral water that I placed by the bed as a weapon—it was looking increasingly likely I wouldn't need it for self defense.

Though Koval's handshake was firm, he struggled to look me in the eye. "I'm not a horrible person," he said, apparently having no patience for pleasantries or small talk. "I don't know how I let it get this far. I love my wife, and now that she knows what I've been up to, I'm afraid she'll leave me. She's not into any of that racist stuff. I know it sounds ridiculous that I thought I could keep something this huge from her. I did it because I know how dangerous the people in Atomwaffen are. How could I *not* keep her out of it?"

I understood his dilemma. I had also refused to mix personal and business affairs or get my wife and children involved in the movement for fear of "dirtying" them with a mind-set and lifestyle that deep down I knew was toxic. I realized my mistakes too late for my own good. They left me after I failed to prioritize them over the movement-centric ICP I was too afraid to lose. My wife cut ties and drifted to safety with our two children, causing me to sink deeper.

Koval nodded. He said, "I love her. She's the one good thing in my life. I never wanted to—"

"Bring hate home?" I acknowledged.

For the next two hours, Koval spilled his guts, and it felt more like a marriage counseling session than an extremist intervention. The more I listened and asked him to examine the factors that led him to where he was now, the more openly he reflected and spoke about his failures. He talked about his experiences inside Atomwaffen, and even then I saw the broken child who was hiding behind the monster that attended a hate training camp and taught racists to kill. What revealed itself was not someone into Satanic rituals, Charles Manson, Hitler, or murder— or even violence for that matter—but a frightened young man who mistakenly sought refuge in the most dangerous place imaginable and could not find his way out.

Before Koval could move on, however, he needed his life to be stable—not again but for the first time. I would not let him off the hook for all the damage he caused. I couldn't do that. Despite my understanding of the broken child hiding beneath the veneer of a monster, accountability and meaningful atonement are critical to the healing process, and Koval had a lot of atoning to do.

But that would come in time. Helping stabilize him in his time of crisis and ensuring his family's safety needed to happen first. Without those securities in place, there was a higher risk of losing him. Having seen others tuck tail and run back to their old lives when the going got tough, I understood the risk of pushing too hard. If faced with too much to overcome at once, it can seem easier to suppress the discomfort by diving back into a familiar role rather than doing the difficult work required for progress to occur. I decided not to press Koval, yet.

I urged him again to contact authorities if he knew anything about a threat of violence.

His eyes implored me to lighten up.

"They need to know immediately if there any imminent threats. Otherwise, it comes crashing back down on you."

He pondered it as if estimating the numbers of fibers in the carpet. Then he shook his head. "No, nothing like that. No plans. They wouldn't tell me anyway. I'm too new."

I knew he wasn't telling me everything. It would take time before he trusted I wasn't out to get him, and that I was just concerned about public safety.

"Okay," I said, taking another sip from my water bottle and considering the tricky situation. "What about those maps of the power grid you claimed you could get? If you have them, you need to turn them over to authorities before I can help you. I'm not interested in shielding you from prosecution for a crime you're guilty of. If you have them or gave them to someone else, you need to tell the FBI right now."

"Yeah, I know," Koval said. He squeezed his knee tightly with his hand, working a cramping muscle. "I kind of lied about having access to the maps. I felt like I needed to have some skin in the game with Atomwaffen. I think they're as pissed at me as the FBI are."

We agreed we were on the same page. If I found out he misled me, I would walk and leave him to deal with the repercussions of his choices on his own. He saw I was sticking my neck out for him, and every instinct told me Koval was sincere and ashamed of what he'd done.

We established a *link* between us. Going forward, he saw me as trustworthy and there to help him. In return, he committed to change. Had he not bought into the process, any subsequent steps in his disengagement would have been difficult to achieve.

I knew going in that it would be a long and grueling road for Koval. But if it meant one less terrorist on the street with the means to hurt innocent people, I would walk it with him and hold his hand the whole way if he needed me to.

Koval's journey is one we're still traveling together, but these days the horizon doesn't look as far off as it once did. He understands I cannot carry him—only he can grapple with his past and work to make amends with those he harmed—but he was grateful I showed him an off-ramp from his dead-end road. I promised to stick around until he found his way home. I'm proud to report that almost three years later, Koval has stayed on track. His wife appreciates it, too.

# 16

## Filter Out the White Noise

### Step Two: Listen
#### *Omar*

*Listening to extremists requires thick skin, self-control, and patience, allowing them to be first to articulate emotions, intents, and goals in leaving extremism behind. Authentic listening requires one to filter out ideological noise and hyperbole to identify the pre-radicalization potholes that detoured them and which factors may have motivated the adoption of extremist behaviors.*

LEBANESE AMERICAN WRITER AND POET Khalil Gibran wrote, "Listen not to what he says, but what he does not say." The Beatles sang for us to "whisper words of wisdom." I cannot think of better advice for those seeking to help someone from their path of radicalization, since heavy-handed or disingenuous approaches make extremists skittish and paranoid. It was Gibran's wisdom that helped me with Omar, a Belgian Muslim who'd just returned home to Brussels after being imprisoned for fighting in Syria for the so-called Islamic State (ISIS).

While I have focused this book primarily on white-supremacist extremism in the United States, hate and violent extremism are transnational and come in many forms. Because the human psyche does not change from region to region, country to country, continent to continent, or person to person, the reasons that different people around the world succumb to extremist narratives remain similar: the need to fulfill ICP is ubiquitous, and potholes are both nonpartisan and, if not maintained with vigilance, equal-opportunity destroyers.

Beyond any fundamental doctrinal differences between the various extremist movements operating globally today, they all share one cruel, underlying aim: to seduce vulnerable people through the manipulation and exploitation of their fear, pain, and uncertainty into adopting values that falsely inspire hope in a less miserable and more meaningful life. Savvy extremist propagandists will always attempt to capitalize on a situation where dissent or uncertainty exists. Given that, I shouldn't have been surprised when I agreed to help Omar—a first-generation son of immigrants who was swept up into fighting for ISIS—disengage after he returned home from fighting in Syria, as I found so much of his story familiar to my own.

While I didn't have to do much filtering of ideological noise with Omar—he was already very self-aware that what he did was wrong—I provided the only friendly ears aside from his wife to listen to him talk through his struggles with disengagement. Despite the differences in our extremist movements, the road of redemption (and its winding twists and turns) for formers is universal.

Omar found me while watching the local TV news in Brussels. A reporter was covering the meetings I organized with members of the Muslim community on the outskirts of the city in Vilvoorde—a town hit by ISIS-related youth radicalization. When Omar reached out, I was still in Belgium for a few more days. He asked his probation officer to help arrange an in-person meeting with me, and I agreed without hesitation.

We met outside my hotel in downtown Brussels late the following evening, after Omar finished his double shift extruding and twisting wire for clothing hangers in a factory across town. Following his release from prison six months prior, it was the only work he could find, despite his college engineering degree and a solid work history.

By 2012, Belgium, a small European country about the size of the US state of Maryland, with a population of just over eleven million, had become Europe's largest per capita pipeline of men and women swearing allegiance to the ISIS.* It troubled Omar's Muslim community for several important reasons—because of the violence that those who joined ISIS might commit back home and for the safety and future of their peaceful enclave in Belgium. Of the estimated three hundred young people who left Belgium to fight in Syria and Iraq, only Omar and three others have ever returned home alive.

In 2010, five years before Omar stumbled upon a radical Islamist narrative, a firebrand named Fouad Belkaçem—recognized by Belgian authorities as one of the most dangerous ISIS recruiters in the country—had set up shop in Antwerp with a group he called Sharia4Belgium. Before the rise of ISIS, the charismatic Belkaçem—known to his associates by his nom de guerre, Abu Imran—played a vital role in the early radicalization of young Belgian Muslims to Islamist mujahideen. Now that ISIS had its bloody grip on the black banner and was waving it across Iraq and Syria, it was a natural segue for Belkaçem to rally support for his jihad among disenfranchised Belgian Muslims and the displaced Muslim refugees living among them. The same bitterness and resentment I felt as a first-generation American growing up in Chicago was the same one shared by many young sons and daughters of Muslim émigrés in Belgium who felt displaced and rejected by the dominant cultures of their new home—including Omar. Jobs were hard to find, and Muslims were a marginalized minority group, often segregated into ethnic and religious ghettos. With his well-crafted exploitation of the growing disenfranchisement among young immigrant Muslims and the support of ISIS behind him, Belkaçem quickly gathered strength in numbers.

---

* P. Van Ostaeyen, "Belgian Radical Networks and the Road to the Brussels Attacks," *CTC Sentinel,* 2016.

In 2010, Belkaçem announced to a crowd gathered outside a courthouse in Antwerp, "Tyranny and corruption in this country have prevailed; economic crises, pedophilia, crime, growing Islamophobia. As in the past, we [Muslims] have saved Europe from the dark ages. We now plan to do the same." He described how he had "the right solution for all crises," calling upon his followers to "implement Sharia law in Belgium." Although Belkaçem made this statement in Belgium in 2010, it could have easily come from Clark Martell, the neo-Nazi skinhead who recruited me into his white-power skinhead movement in a dark alley in 1987. Extremist firebrands—be they Islamist mullahs, anti-government sovereign citizens, religious fundamentalists, the Klan, white nationalists, skinheads, or cult leaders—operate on the same black-and-white unidimensional plane: where those enticed by their doctrines live in a paradoxical state of being permanently under threat (but somehow still the greatest "thing" ever), and in the face of such devastating risk, survival becomes reduced to an "us" or "them" narrative.

A first-generation Belgian Muslim of Moroccan immigrant parents, Omar was one of the first of many young people to fall for Belkaçem's lies.

Omar's story, despite its dark trajectory, was also tinged with moments of humor and gratitude. We met on a public bench outside my hotel, underneath a tree that seemed to house a hundred birds. Being surrounded by a steady stream of foot traffic put me at ease about this first-time encounter. With chubby cheeks and a genuine, guileless smile, Omar could have passed for a teenager even though he was in his mid-twenties. The dark curls on his head fell below the edge of his Yankees baseball cap. When he smiled, his teeth were straight and white. Only his eyes showed me the pain he carried throughout his young life and how much his struggles had cost him.

Some of what Omar told me were firsthand accounts of Belkaçem's strategies, familiar to me only through my cursory research. He explained how Belkaçem had recruited disillusioned and idealistic young men and women and diverted them with promises of "paradise" and "glory," stressing the reward and meaning they would receive for giving themselves up for the cause. The skinhead who recruited me used the same tactic, purposefully avoiding the word *exchange* as part of the devil's bargain, because if one thought of joining an extremist cause as a two-way deal, leaders would shun them as greedy traitors or apostates. Those in extremist movements are expected to give of themselves and receive only abstractions like pride and glory in return for a lifetime of blind devotion.

Despite a chemical engineering degree from a respected Belgian university, a decent salary when he worked in a medical laboratory, and a joyful marriage with his childhood sweetheart who was expecting their first child, Omar found little else in the way of support in Belgium.

Then, someone defaced the mosque with anti-Muslim slurs where he and his pregnant wife prayed. A faux Molotov cocktail was left on the doorstep to punctuate the sentiment. The Muslim community in Brussels felt isolated after the incident, afraid. Omar was beyond feeling isolated, he was angry and out for blood. He fumed that someone dared to attack his family and his faith. Only words had been left behind this time, he thought, but what would come next from the Westerners who hated his God and brown skin? Violence? Death? "There will be no next time," Omar promised his wife.

The Molotov cocktail left outside Omar's mosque was not what propelled him into extremism but merely the final straw. His lifelong pursuit for a purposeful identity became clouded when he most needed clarity to protect and comfort his family. Omar's passionate idealism, compounded by feelings of marginalization since youth, along with the overwhelming stigma he carried for feeling "different," is what drove him far from reason. Just shy of twenty-four years old, Omar answered the fiery cleric's call and went to Syria to fight for the ISIS, where, unlike in Brussels, he felt he belonged. His younger brother, Sam, and two of their neighborhood mates traveled with him. They were afraid of the prospect of war but excited at the same time, believing that what they were doing—waging jihad in the name of Allah—was something of a "humanitarian mission." Being fooled into saving something of great value rang true in my ex-skinhead ears. I was led to feel the same about a coming "race war"—that it was not about hate but instead rooted in a deep love for a dying culture worth saving and risking everything for.

The four young men piled into Omar's sedan—squeezing between the supplies they were asked to bring along—and they drove for six days across Central Europe to join their brothers fighting to reclaim the soul of Islam.

"The rusty red beast barely ran in Brussels traffic," Omar reminisced in perfect English, dropping only the subtlest hints he started life as a Moroccan Arabic speaker and only became a Belgian French speaker by necessity. "How we made it from our housing complex in the suburbs outside of Brussels through five countries and into Turkey in that automobile *de merde* was thanks only to Allah, praise be unto him," he said, letting out a sharp laugh that faded quickly. "When they released me from prison, I'm not sure why, but the only other thing I missed besides my brother, was that stupid car."

When Omar, Youssef, Salah, and Sam arrived in Turkey, they met up with a larger group of young men. Two women—a white university student from Norway and a young girl from Tunisia, whom Omar guessed were both around his same age—had also joined ranks. The group loaded into a box van and received instructions to switch vehicles at predetermined waypoints every fifty kilometers along the route to the Syrian border to avoid detection from Turkish authorities. Once they were within a day's walk from their meeting point, their driver handed them off to a local scout who took them to a transfer station at Kilis and then on to Raqqa, where they proceeded on foot to the first camp.

Instead of the one-day walk that was described to them, it took the group two days because the young women struggled to carry the men's food rations and the extra ammunition they might need to fight along the way. Like their white-supremacist counterparts and other cult-like movements, radicalized Islamists—militants who advocate for violence-based Islamic fundamentalism—only place women onto a pedestal when trying to sell the outside world on the "benevolent" mission of their cause, or to persuade women about the perks of joining, any benefit being a blatant untruth. The actual treatment of women by men in extremist environments, once new female recruits are ushered in with reverence and indoctrinated on the importance of the sacred female vessel for the future of *X-Y-Z* warrior tribe, points to a very different tale of misogyny, abuse, rape, and the tragic universality of toxic masculinity.

ISIS leaders offered Omar and the new recruits vague promises to get them to come to Syria to fight. Most had a contact on the inside who instructed them directly as they made their way across the desert, keeping them anxious and excited about what awaited them.

Broken up over two scorching-hot October days, the walk was, as Omar described, "almost a meditation." They did it in complete silence—except for the serenade of improvised a cappella pop songs Sam sang to liven up their somber moods before being told to stop by their handler.

Omar held back tears behind a forced smile as he recounted, "I think a few of the older Dutch fighters wanted to shoot Sam by the time we met up in Aleppo with al-Nusra Front."

After the recruits arrived at camp and received their Russian assault rifles, commanders welcomed them with a feast. With no guidance once the celebration ended, they were left to their own devices to do what they thought was expected of them.

Omar was made to wait at the camp for five months before he received orders for the battlefield. During that time, he drove a truck and moved supplies between two quiet outposts that saw little action. Sam and their two friends returned to Raqqa for the time being, reloading the ammunition they received from Russian militias and restocking supply lines from the home base.

Sam was told to organize village shakedowns. Even though he was only nineteen, they tasked him with the role of identifying villagers suspected of petty theft or rounding up those who were found guilty of the crime of "free thinking" against the Islamic State. The work unsettled Sam enough that he lied to Omar about his role for weeks.

Then, after allegedly overhearing Sam tell his mother over the phone that he was planning to leave and return home to Brussels, the man leading Sam's regiment—his emir—another Belgian Muslim, executed Sam while he was asleep in his tent. He was the first of their group to die.

Omar's boyhood friends Youssef and Salah died two weeks after Sam, killed by rocket fire from Syrian government forces. When the news of their deaths reached Omar, it shattered him. He spent several weeks alone, going through the motions, fending for himself, before attempting his escape from the camp.

"I was so bloody scared," Omar told me. "We all were. From the moment we stepped foot in Syria and for the next five months, we were terrified. Then, suddenly, everyone but me was dead—maybe we weren't afraid enough."

Omar broke eye contact, locking his stare on to something beyond me. I knew enough not to turn around to look. There would be nothing to see. "They made Sam and his unit set up roadblocks in town and demand ransoms from the people they caught," he continued, "and when someone couldn't pay, they cut off their hands."

I recognized the blankness on Omar's face—the detached retreat from the pain of a traumatic experience—because it is the same look most former white supremacists I work with also wear when talking about their memories. For years after I denounced the movement, I caught myself in the mirror with the same lifeless eyes, staring far beyond my reflection, lost in a jumble of raw memories that overcame me and drew me deeper inside myself. Omar's intense guilt over the deaths of his brother and two friends, which he blamed himself for, drove him to contemplate suicide. Even while he talked about how lucky he considered himself to be, his palpable disquiet, along with the mood swings he described, were hallmarks of PTSD.

His first attempt to escape nearly got him killed. When one of his commanders saw him in the village bartering with a young boy, offering his ammunition for an old moped, he called Omar into his post that night to ask why he was in town when he should have been at camp.

"I knew enough to lie," Omar said. "I saw what happened to Sam. I said the boy gave me some trouble when I tried to confiscate his moped to move supplies faster. I told him I showed the boy how many bullets I would put in his skull if he didn't hand it over." Although Omar's commander accepted his excuse, he put guards on high alert to keep an eye on him.

After waiting another two months, Omar made his second attempt and was able to ditch his unit. "It took a while to get away but I managed to steal two American Express cards from the camp accountant," he recalled. "One night, after everyone was tired from training all day in the sun, I slipped away through town and walked seventy kilometers to the border and into Turkey. I was afraid and exhausted when I arrived two days later. I maxed out one credit card to pay a taxi driver to take me fifteen hours to Istanbul and used the other to buy food and a one-way plane ticket to Brussels and a soccer ball for my son to grow up with. Then I flushed the cards down the toilet in a hostel."

Omar knew enough to give himself over to police once he returned home to Belgium.

His wife, Miriam, met him at the airport to introduce him to his son for the first time before police took him into custody. "I held them both in my arms and gave them a farewell kiss on their foreheads, then I walked into the airport security office and told them to arrest me because I was a terrorist. The only way to move past it would be to first face up to what I had done."

Listening to Omar tell me about his journey, I could see his call to radicalization answered three questions that eluded him his entire life: *Who am I? Where do I belong?* and *What does my life mean?*

Like I had, Omar also felt invisible before finding his movement. His cause made him feel like he was *somebody,* a hero if he would join the fight against those he believed were keeping him and his family down. Feeling rejected by the greater community in Brussels after the vandalism of his mosque, Omar found his tribe in ISIS—his new family. He belonged *with* them and *to* them. His movement, like most extremist movements, expected supporters to pay the price of admission and do what was necessary to remain integral to the cause, to protect the mission from outsiders through violence.

"Going back to the person I was before joining ISIS wasn't an option," Omar told me. "That's what our oppressors and the traitors wanted. We had to kill all links to the old 'us' that might pull us back. If anyone tried to leave, ending their life became a priority." I suspected this was for the same reasons that white extremists also operated in this way—once someone shamed the "family" and pulled the curtain back for the world to see the truth behind their lies and corruption, if discrediting them with more lies didn't work, they would have no choice but to destroy them. It rarely got to the point of physically killing deserters, though it happens, but metaphorically, the reputational "deaths" attributed to extremism are infinite.

Within Omar's new community of true believers, he no longer felt lost or weary from the tiresome burden of not knowing what had kept him marginalized when he saw other Moroccans and Muslims who seemed to love life in Brussels. When Fouad Belkaçem issued a challenge for Belgian Muslims to wake up and submit to Sharia law or face dire consequences, Omar listened. He saw it as his duty to draw victimhood like a dagger and press it against the throats of his oppressors; to become a warrior for a great cause—a martyr, even.

I told Omar I was here to help him through his transition—though he accomplished disengagement on his own, he still needed an aftercare network. He would not be isolated anymore. It was important for Omar to understand he was not alone. I reminded him there were many happy and healthy formers out in the real world who would also help him, if he would let them.

"I lost my younger brother, too," I said. "After I left the movement, a gang member shot and killed him—Buddy—over drugs. Other formers helped me get through it when it happened. I guess it's why I do what I do now. Be everyone's big brother, I guess."

"Yeah?" Omar said, wiping his cheeks. "I'm sorry to hear about Buddy."

"I know what it's like to blame yourself for it, too."

We spent hours sitting on that bench together, shouldering each other's devastation for not having been able to protect our younger brothers—for letting them down when we should have raised them up. We stitched up each other's tattered souls, oblivious to time and the boulevard noise around us, and we vowed to stop blaming ourselves for their deaths. That we would keep our new surrogacy alive and turn our guilt into positive action, so no more kid brothers would die for foolish causes.

Perhaps embarrassed to be tearing up in front of the tattooed white man he sought out through his probation officer, Omar wiped his cheek and steadied himself. My sleeve had also grown soggy.

"I thought we were the good guys fighting evil—that we were saving the world."

"Me, too, Omar," I echoed. "Most of us did at one point. Even Sam and your friends." I embraced my new brother.

Omar took his first step toward redemption by acknowledging that his actions had contributed to tragedy. Although his past would always haunt him, the pain would lessen as he repaired his potholes—one by one, over time. Omar hoped that one day he could allow himself to appreciate the joys of his fortunate life and help fix some of the problems that funnel young people into extremism. He holds on to the hope that one day he can help others in his community replace the radical propaganda of ISIS with the true peaceful teachings of Islam.

It was getting late and I didn't want Omar tired for his early work shift—he still had a long ride home ahead of him. I rose from the bench and offered my hand to pull him up. It was then, from an adjacent service drive, that a stray mutt strutted up and sauntered between us.

With a piercing shriek, Omar leaped clear off the sidewalk and up onto the bench.

"What are you doing, Omar?" I asked.

"Dogs are bad luck!" he said, glancing around, gathering himself before stepping down off the bench.

"What are you talking about?" I tried not to laugh and embarrass him. "You just screamed and jumped as high as I did when I was a little boy and a harmless baby garter snake crawled over my shoe. I cried then, too. But I was six!"

"Dogs scare me, brother!" Omar confessed. He was smiling now. "I didn't grow up with them."

"I haven't seen someone jump that high since the days of Michael Jordan," I said. We chuckled. The dog came back toward us and rolled over onto its back, and I scratched its stomach. Tentative, Omar quietly crouched down beside me.

"Pet it. There's nothing to be afraid of—other than fleas or maybe rabies," I joked. "Just another lonely soul wandering the streets tonight." Omar seemed to enjoy the dog's enthusiasm, and as he rubbed its belly it shimmied in delight. Still, when a bird caught its attention and it leaped, Omar again went soaring into the air.

Locals took notice of the two odd men on a bench playing with a stray dog. We laughed, trying to imagine what they thought we were jumping around for in the middle of the night.

"How did a white boy like you never end up in prison like me?" Omar asked as he hailed a cab at the curb.

*Privilege.* The thought entered my mind, ashamed by this difference between us, and the times I deserved a jail cell that never found me because of my skin color and the benefit of my parents' bail money.

"Luck," I responded, holding back on the truth, unable to find the courage to be honest. I suppose I felt the weight of knowing how difficult it would be for Omar, not only to break through his stigma and feel welcome in his own community again but to convince every white face he would encounter for the rest of his days that he wasn't a terrorist anymore. Perhaps Omar knew this, too, but he showed no signs of fearing it.

"*As-salaam-alaikum,* Christian," he said.

"*Wa-alaikum-salaam,* buddy," I replied, pulling a fresh pack of cigarettes from my coat. The stress of battling Russian trolls in the prior months had gotten to me. I relapsed in a weak moment, as America's heating rhetoric was also driving what appeared to be an increase in extremist violence *and* the number of people reaching out to me for help in the wake of the Unite the Right rally in Charlottesville. Omar's taxi pulled up. "Make sure and give your baby boy Sammy a kiss from his new American uncle," I said, waving.

"You know, Christian," Omar called out as he stepped into the back seat of the taxi, "those cigarettes will kill you faster than a Soviet Kalashnikov."

"We can't have that now, can we?" I replied, stuffing the half-opened smokes back into my pocket and bidding farewell to my new friend. I was disappointed in myself for having started smoking again. What began as one cigarette two months earlier had become a full-blown habit again.

It would have crushed my wife, Britton, if she found out I picked it up again, so I struggled with how to come clean with her. I imprudently hid it until I could figure out how to quit on my own and promised myself I would stop soon. *What better time than now?* I wondered.

As soon as Omar pulled out of sight, though, I unwrapped the pack to enjoy one final cigarette before ditching the smokes and shutting down for the night.

*One last one won't kill me,* I thought, pulling the lighter from my jacket pocket.

As I turned my body to avoid the breeze and light the cigarette dangling from my lips, the worn-down sole of my sneaker caught the smooth edge of the hotel's brass curb, and I slipped, tumbling flat onto my back. Lucky for me, Omar was far enough down the boulevard to miss my impromptu performance of *The Nutcracker.* There I lay, alone on the cobblestone, flat on my back. It bruised my ego worse than my tailbone before the poetic justice of the broken cigarette resting between my fingers dawned on me.

Not lost one bit was the fact that quitting smoking was a lot like disengaging from extremism—both are highly addictive, and even folks that have stopped can be led back if new potholes appear or old ones are not properly addressed. Sometimes, having someone to remind you of the negative impacts of life's choices, or the emotional stress of knowing you're hiding something from those you care about, can help you stay a more positive course.

I got up and dusted myself off, ditching the remnants of my crooked cigarette and the rest of the pack in a trash bin.

"What doesn't kill you makes you stronger," I reasoned.

# 17

## Mapping the Journey

### Step 3: Learn
### *Ben*

*After establishing trust, identify potholes and evaluate which outside options exist to repair them—these "off-ramps" strengthen a person's resilience and help them establish a positive support network to achieve lasting disengagement. Since potholes are only part of what steer people toward extremism, it's also important to help individuals learn how to develop positive identity, community, and purpose (ICP).*

W HEN BEN—THE PAROLED WAR VETERAN who embraced extremism in prison after alcohol and drugs stopped numbing the pain of losing his friends in Iraq—emailed me for help, I could have turned my back on him. But I'm glad I didn't.

> *I was hoping you might have some time to talk. I'm trying to move away from the alt-right and hoped you might have some advice. It has affected my family and I just want to make things right. If you can, please email me back. Thanks.*
>
> —Ben

After the video of Ben's Denver street brawl went viral on Facebook, he became somewhat of a well-known figure of the alt-right. In his video interviews following the altercation, I saw something in him that reminded me of myself during my misspent youth. He seemed motivated by something other than hate. I overcame my hesitancy and agreed to meet with him, more curious about him than convinced he was being genuine.

After two months of email and phone correspondence, I knew I made the right choice to mentor Ben. He was tortured and insecure, bright, shy, idealistic, and committed to becoming a force for good in the world—but with no idea how.

When we finally found time to meet in person, I watched as Ben pulled up in his Chevy pickup tricked out with a diamond-plate toolbox bolted in the bed and his Saint Bernard, Stanley, hanging his tongue to lap up the passing breeze. We met in the parking lot of a coffee shop next to a megachurch alongside a single-lane Arizona highway, the place we agreed to as a midpoint between Yuma and the cabin I rented for a writing retreat.

Ben hopped out of the truck but left Stanley behind in the cab, rubbing his dog's head through the open window and feeding him a treat before making his way over to me. A tall, gruff-looking roughneck with a full beard, Ben appeared different from the photos I saw of him online. Happy, maybe. He smiled as he approached, a skip in his step. I wondered if he had grown the beard to fully embrace farm life or to hide his face. I reminded myself to whisper words of wisdom, not judge or debate him.

Inside the quaint café, comfy couches sat nestled inside of nooks and leaflets for Christian youth retreats laid scattered on the tables. Thankfully, the coffee was bolder than the religious propaganda. The loud whirring noise of the espresso grinder gave us the perfect cover to speak freely on a corner sofa without having to worry too much about eavesdroppers.

We talked, and I found Ben to be a decent man. If I hadn't known him by his short-lived media persona, I might have called him a friend without thinking twice. He was humble, smart, and funny, and he genuinely stressed about the chaos happening in the world around him.

We talked for three hours like we were old friends catching up, not once touching on ideology or politics. I waited for Ben to bring up his disengagement, and finally, he did.

"I never meant to hurt anyone," he said in a refrain I commonly hear—one motivated by a productive sense of guilt that needs addressing.

"But you did," I added gently.

"Things spiraled out of control," he said, "and I got sucked in fast. After a while, I had no interest in the people I found myself surrounded with."

I nodded, relating to his moment of clarity. He thought his racist actions were helping make the world better, just like I believed thirty years before. Now, he was going through the same anxiety I developed after realizing how wrong I was.

"I supported the cause," he added, "because I thought poor whites were being underrepresented and the media was pushing a 'white guilt' agenda. I just wanted to say my piece about it."

Ben said he wasn't a Nazi, and I believed him. His grandfather had fought against the Germans and liberated Jews from the concentration camps during the Second World War. Ben also fought bravely for his country. But once he joined ranks with the "ex-" skinheads who made up the European Heritage Front, the Nazi association stuck. It rubbed off on him, and he accepted the label.

"It's my fault. The rush of it all got to my head, and I fucked up. Again."

I knew the shame from where he spoke.

I had also felt powerless and embraced a deception that filled me with a sense of empowerment, only to fall and become crushed under the weight of what I'd done. I wasn't a war veteran, but the feeling of control, the violence to justify it, and the power to make demands of others in a hierarchy was addictive to my teenage mind.

But Ben was almost thirty years old when he was swept up by the alt-right. I was curious about what pushed him that late in life. As we talked about prison, his time in Iraq, and his two friends killed in action, the pieces of the puzzle fell into place. He'd also brought home, it turned out, an all-too-common souvenir of war: PTSD.

"Some days my mind feels 100 percent disabled," he confided, his voice shaky. "It just won't work to control my anger—feels like bottle rockets going off in my head when I open my eyes."

I observed signs of Ben's PTSD throughout our conversation—when he trailed off during a long, detailed description of events on the battlefield, how he studiously avoided stories of his friends' deaths like improvised explosives. When I posed questions designed to shed more light on his potholes, he tensed up, just like I imagine he did in Fallujah when civilian vehicles passed alongside his Humvee.

Ben was in pain and struggling. He was physically fit, articulate, insightful, and remorseful about what he'd done, but he was hurting. More than once, he referred to himself as "damaged goods," who never knew when another severe episode of the "fuck-its" would land on him like a ton of bricks. It was in those raw moments, during his despair of feeling worthless, that he said he always made the wrong choices. It sent Ben to war twice and prison once. He couldn't muster the courage, he said, to pull the trigger on his gun when he'd put the barrel in his mouth, or the half dozen times he washed down a bottle of pills with whiskey only to shove his fingers down his throat and puke them all up. He feared someday he would give in to his wish to end it all. That's when I noticed the tremor in his hand.

He told me what family life was like on the farm—about the birth father he never met, an "old civil rights hippie" who taught a course on '60s counterculture at a community college in Florida. And he told me about his sister, who disowned him when word got out about Ben's white-nationalist activities.

He didn't say it in so many words but Ben's openness gave me the opportunity to learn what really drove him off course. More than anything else, his impressive drive to make an impact in society and the emotional and psychological potholes of war and prison, perhaps even growing up feeling abandoned by his birth father, had detoured him to the fringes to find peace. From there, once the taste of "paradise" that the movement promised rested on his lips, ambition took hold, and he sunk his teeth in.

Society had punished him for his crimes, not only with prison but also by stigmatizing Ben in a way he felt he could never shake. Even though he accepted responsibility for his actions, he felt no one would remember him for his proud service to his country. His allegiance to hate would be his legacy, he felt, and now that he wanted to transcend it and start building a normal life, society wouldn't allow it. Posters calling Ben a Nazi showed up plastered on telephone poles in his home town months after he disengaged and while he was still contemplating how to repair the damage he'd caused. His lifelong neighbors began avoiding him. Police made extra patrols to his isolated homestead. He felt cornered with no way out.

I understand the value of shunning bad behavior as a deterrent and social corrective for the harmful urges humans exhibit. We must confront hate wherever we see it and punish those who've committed violent crimes, that much I agree with. I also believe that violent or hateful people should not fully enjoy the benefits of a peaceful society until they are willing to hold themselves accountable for the damage they have caused. But while an individual is assessing the actions necessary to maintain their accountability, we must allow space for rehabilitation and growth to occur or we risk adopting the same type of intolerance extremists are guilty of.

We must be careful to not become so blind in our opposition of hate that we embody the very things we hope to eradicate. In an era where moral arguments often play out over social media, this can be difficult. Where extreme judgment thrives, or what some call *virtue signaling*—a pejorative for the expression of moral values with little substance beyond words to back it up—it can sometimes prove impossible.

Too many times, I see sincere individuals who are hoping to abandon their extremist mind-set get shoved back into the arms of ideology by "anti-hate" activists who subscribe to a social punishment–oriented philosophy of boycotting past indiscretions as irredeemable sins—a "cancel culture" that is itself extreme in its rigidity and lack of nuance. After making initial progress in leaving hate behind, others have disappeared on me and gone deeper underground when faced with this stigma, leaving them unable to work through their demons and make amends.

Ben first landed in the crosshairs of activists as an early promoter of the Charlottesville Unite the Right rally. Four months before the rally, though, Ben pulled out. He quit his group, telling other members he needed to repair an embattled relationship with his fiancée. He was afraid to tell his comrades, those who were going in part due to his efforts, that he was having daily gut checks about his involvement and concerns about where his life was heading. As the rally neared, Ben faded away, only to be reawakened by chants of "Blood and soil!"—a slogan Ben borrowed from the Third Reich and suggested to his group months earlier. In that way, he was there that day—men carried through the actions he helped set into motion. Watching his friends on the news as they marched down the street with tiki torches, Ben knew he was partly responsible for the violence that erupted.

After the Charlottesville rally, one of Ben's friends from another alt-right group, who couldn't shake his guilt by association over Heather Heyer's murder, committed suicide. Ben said that hit him hard.

"I probably fucked him up. I should have seen he wasn't all in and told him not to go. After he heard about the woman dying at the rally, he went home and shot himself." Ben paused, looking out at Stanley licking dirt off the half-drawn truck window. "It's like I fed the bullet into the chamber of his gun." It was clear he felt he had let another brother down—another soldier who paid for Ben's mistake with his life.

When Ben told me that he reconnected with one of his old professors from a gender studies course he'd taken after his release from prison, I was surprised, to say the least, wondering what interest a white nationalist would have in gender studies. I listened as he told me about wanting to go back to school to finish his college degree. Ben was still searching, even after he thought he found his purpose in white nationalism. Though he had been an effective college campus recruiter for the alt-right while enrolled, Ben also wanted to learn more, to understand different perspectives.

His professor, a transgender man of color—something that didn't seem to bother Ben—hadn't known about Ben's politics or his notoriety until the school kicked Ben off campus after anti-fascist activists revealed his identity in the wake of the violent Denver rally video. Ben didn't put up a fight. He immediately withdrew from classes and sank deeper into the movement instead of continuing to expand his worldview.

A year later, the same professor reached out to Ben to tell him it was unfortunate to not have him in class. Even though he only learned about Ben's views after his expulsion, he wanted to tell him he appreciated his attentiveness, his willingness to learn, and the considerate non-derogatory essays he had submitted. Sad to see Ben go, the professor apologized for taking so long to track him down and pass along the feedback. Ben's old professor then invited him to meet in person. He had a special request.

Ben could have decided it was easier to dive headfirst back into the movement—he was at the peak of his extremist activity—instead of facing the consequences of his actions. Repairing the harm he caused? That was a mountain we were both still unsure how to climb. I assured him that if he would try, I would help—and life would get better in time—so long as he remained genuine, I said. Lying or dishonesty would end our deal.

Before even meeting Ben, I had already broken my golden rule: "Don't judge, just help." After the whirlwind of destruction that I created during my eight years in the white-supremacist movement—double the time Ben spent—how could *I* judge *him?* I had no right to assume the higher moral ground. I went in with a preconception of who Ben was. I manufactured my assumptions based on the limited knowledge I had absorbed from the media. We spoke on the phone and kept in frequent text communication but I assumed I already knew him when I met him for the first time. It was a mistake on my part.

Several times during our coffeehouse meeting, I reached too far trying to pinpoint what motivated Ben to adopt extremism.

"Was it seeing your friends die in Iraq? That must have been horrible and traumatic. May be the PTSD?" I pried. "Did the Aryan Brotherhood or Hammerskins recruit you in prison?" My curiosity bordered on analytical evaluation. Not only was it something I wasn't qualified for, I wasn't aware I was doing it. After the first thirty minutes of me bombarding Ben with pointed questions, sometimes answering them myself before allowing him to, I noticed he started clamming up. He was eyeing his dog, Stanley, outside in the truck. I apologized when I realized I was out of line. That's when Ben told me he'd read every psychology book in the prison library at least three times, and I lost him when I misdiagnosed his "nihilism" as "determinism." He was as much of an aspiring criminal profiler as I was. We both laughed about it later.

It wasn't until I allowed myself to step into Ben's perspective and I let him lead me through his story, that I truly *learned* about his potholes. Though they included PTSD and the trauma of war and prison, they mostly stemmed from his isolation as a kid and his genuine wonder and ambition to do good in the world. He also admitted a history of getting sidetracked. He kept referring to attacks of the fuck-its, where he would lose hope in humanity for prolonged periods that could last from a day to several weeks. It was in those moments when Ben felt his mind was "disabled"—and he was most susceptible to problematic behavior.

It was also important to experience Ben's understanding of what he thought he needed to progress in a healthy and sustainable way. To be honest, neither of us knew the best way for him to move forward. The renewed academic relationship with his former professor was a great way to engage Ben in exploring new ICP, but his mental well-being concerned us both. He agreed to let me help him find a trauma specialist.

Paying close attention to which potholes led Ben to his choices, his motivations for them, and the regret and shame he felt for his behavior, helped inform me as to which resources he needed to move away from self-loathing and toward empathy and forgiveness—for his victims and for himself.

I connected Ben with a PTSD specialist, a neuroscientist in Sweden, and a therapist back home in Yuma. He needed to learn how to live with his disorder and not let it disable him. He had quit drinking and taking prescription pills before joining the European Heritage Front (EHF), but with so many life changes and underlying conditions improperly managed, his entire disengagement could swerve off course if we weren't careful.

Ben's old professor asked him to join his team as an assistant researcher for a gender studies research project funded through the university. He now spends a few hours a week gathering data and meeting with them regularly. The strong bond he and his professor developed gave Ben an outlet. His professor, who could have previously fallen victim to violence from Ben and his crew, is someone Ben how confides in about his past without fear of shame or judgment. After six months of working together, Ben found not only a mentor but also a friend.

Ben still had many struggles ahead of him. One of the most difficult was maintaining a meaningful connection to his fiancée, who remains on the other side of an ocean in Iceland. Despite being a member of the women's division of EHF, she had disengaged several months before Ben when she saw the writing on the wall. Extremism was a dead end—for her, for Ben, and everyone else. Hate was easy to spew on the Internet, where it seemed edgy and rebellious, but people were dying in real life. She pledged her allegiance to Ben because she loved him *and* his beliefs, but now she only loved him.

Despite Ben's fiancée's change of heart and her self-driven commitment to make right her negative contributions, authorities would not allow her to leave Iceland and visit her future husband. Flagged persona non grata by US border agents because of Ben, she failed in two attempts to enter the

United States, despite having a spotless record and no prior involvement in violence. And the man she loved couldn't go to her because of his prison record.

While I appreciate the value of accountability, having learned and experienced Ben's detour as best I could, I knew his inability to visit with his fiancée was a major roadblock to his recovery. So, when he asked if I would write a letter of support to immigration control, I agreed. This was not an easy decision, not because I didn't believe what I was writing about Ben but because it forced me to grapple with what Ben represented—someone who once fought *against* the immigration rights of those who deserved it more than he and his fiancée did.

If forgiveness was easy, entire religions wouldn't be based on the notion of it. I reminded myself that if Ben was doing better, it was good for everyone.

I maintain a friendly relationship with Ben. We keep in touch and sometimes message each other with pictures of our loved ones, including Stanley his dog. I enjoyed the photo he snapped with Stanley resting on his lap, which included a snippet of text from a book Ben was reading—*White Fragility: Why It's So Hard to Talk to White People About Racism* by Robin DiAngelo. I replied with a snapshot of me posing with a king cobra in Marrakech's old medina. We all overcome fear in different ways.

As this book goes to press, Ben still hasn't made his exit public, and that's the choice he believes is best for him and his fiancée as they work through their immigration issues. I support his decision but I remain concerned for him and his progress. Since meeting Ben, he has wandered back into the movement at times. While it can be common for individuals to backslide at first, sometimes simply for safety's sake— they may be embedded in a group and not have the proper means to disengage quickly—Ben's obstacles seem to have isolated him further, despite the new connections he made.

Like addiction to an illicit substance, extremist ICP provides a temporary "high" that is hard to resist if redemption seems unattainable. Ben's inability to re-assimilate, or society's unwillingness to allow him to, often proved too difficult a barrier for him to overcome, so he relapsed to his ideological drug for comfort when he faced setbacks. The more Ben went back for a taste, the more challenging his obstacles seemed—until he found himself right back where he started.

Disengaging from extremism is hard, and sometimes it doesn't work. It's important as outsiders that we temper our expectations of the process. When it does work, for most it's a long and grueling road back to humanity. It takes time and the proper resources, both of which Ben had, but also requires patience—which he lacked.

I believe in Ben and respect him as a person. I know he is good when he allows himself to be. Recently, I asked him to think about going public about his struggle disengaging from extremism and to ask for help learning how to make amends. None of us are perfect, I told him, we are human beings who stumble and sometimes fall flat on our face. It's our staring into the sun that blinds us from seeing the road ahead. If progress comes with careful intention, each step we take counts—and so does the occasional pause to rest. What I won't accept is full throttle in reverse gear.

Perhaps it's fear of repercussion—from his friends in the alt-right or enemies on the Left—that makes Ben reluctant to fully disengage. In the meantime, I try not to judge him and instead listen to his ambitions and anxieties, hoping to help him see clearer a little more each time we speak.

# 18

---

## Filling Potholes

### Step Four: Leverage
### *Daniel*

*Leverage outside resources to help individuals build sustainable emotional and behavioral resilience, while also helping them develop positive short- and long-term goals for disengagement. Like emergency "tow trucks," a network of aftercare resources can help achieve those goals, including mental health professionals, counselors and therapists, job trainers, employers and hiring agencies, mentors, educators, life coaches, physicians, faith leaders, clubs, tattoo coverup or laser removal services, other former extremists, or any social service that can help repair relevant potholes—and thus build human resilience—so the focus remains on the individual making healthy progress.*

M Y INTERACTION WITH DANIEL began through his mother, Janet. She reached out to me, desperate to find help for her nineteen-year-old skinhead son. He had come home bruised and bloodied after his new friends used their steel-toed boots and fists to baptize him into the Hammerskin Nation—the same brutal neo-Nazi group I helped lead decades ago.

Janet became alarmed when Daniel arrived to pick her up from her stint in rehab sporting a fresh, homemade swastika tattoo on his right temple, ink he wasn't ashamed to show off to the black nurse who checked them out of the facility.

Janet and I met in a Starbucks in Louisville, Kentucky. She told me about the drug and alcohol addiction she battled until getting herself clean a year earlier. The state revoked her driver's license, so she asked around her Alcoholics Anonymous family for a ride to meet me.

She was nervous when we met. I'd waited outside the café's entrance, every part of me dripping sweat from the blasting heat of the furnace-like Kentucky summer, but she trembled when I shook her hand and shivered when we embraced. Stopping her crying only to praise Jesus, she told me how much it pained her to raise her son in such abject poverty and how she knew she let him down. "I haven't been a good mother," she confessed with a heavy heart.

I guided Janet to a table, and we sat and talked. She told me she loved her children—Daniel and his older sister—and was certain she levied a life sentence on them. She told me how she'd failed her Bible's Golden Rule—*Do unto others as you would have them do unto you*—because she only ever harmed herself and those around her.

"I know I've got to treat others *better* than I've treated myself," she whispered between sniffles, "because Lord knows I ain't ever been so good in the loving-myself department."

I felt her regret, her pain, and her fear—but I also saw Janet's strength. I told her it didn't help for us to continue blaming ourselves for our mistakes—we had to put that energy into making things right, or as close to right as they'll ever be.

*I'm desperate. I don't necessarily want to denounce my ideology but it has done nothing good for me. I feel like I've been a hypocrite for years. Hurting people isn't who I am. I want to be a better person but I don't want to fuck it up. I think you already know my mom, Janet. She says hello. Can you help me? Please.*

—Daniel

Daniel's first message came via Facebook almost a full year after I met Janet, and just two weeks after he returned home from the August 2017 Unite the Right march in Charlottesville. I suspected that Daniel knew his tardiness in waking up from the nightmare he participated in would not win him any favors from me.

But as judgments usually are, mine were off base. He was leery of *my* intentions and all but ignored the open invitation I offered through his mother a year prior. But now, he was desperate.

I flew back to Louisville a few days after receiving his plea. I didn't want him to get second thoughts and risk him changing his mind after exchanging too many words.

Daniel greeted me at his mother's apartment with a "Hey, what's up?" shifting his feet and fidgeting with his hands for some time before extending one to shake mine. Instead of inviting me in, he stepped out on to the landing and shut the door behind him, leading me back down the outdoor concrete steps and to the parking lot.

"Uh, my mom says she's sorry she ain't here. She's at work… somewhere," he said, standing on the sidewalk in front of my rental Jeep. Daniel was not the tough kid I envisioned from the photos his mother shared or the racist ones he posted on his social media accounts, though I suspected that side of him still lingered below the surface. He was tall and beefy, sporting a plain, heather-gray T-shirt beneath a black nylon bomber jacket; his bleached denim pants rolled up a few inches over scuffed, black combat boots. The dishwater-blond hair that poked out in all directions from under his backward ball cap stood in sharp contrast to the bold Nazi tattoos on his face.

I offered Daniel a cigarette. Even though I'd given up smoking several months prior on a trip to Brussels, I kept a pack of Marlboros in my pocket in case I spotted a white nationalist on the street, identifiable by a tattoo or my intuition, to use the ploy of asking for a light as a way of engaging them. Given I don't carry a lighter, the tactic usually works to start a conversation—whether the person smokes or not. It's a trick I learned from Clark Martell, the skinhead who recruited me at fourteen. Offering a smoke in return for their favor gives me the chance to pry without just standing there awkwardly. It's Recruitment 101. Instead of pulling them into my way of thinking, I ask a few pointed questions—and listen. If I listen carefully to their intentions, without losing myself in their words, I typically walk away knowing more about them than they do.

It took three meetings like this with Daniel before he finally let me in and began talking about his traumatic experiences. When he told me he was ready to remove his racist tattoos, including the ones on his face and throat, I was even more encouraged. He'd gotten them to intimidate people, he told me, so they would leave him alone. The tattoos marked him, as his fellow Hammerskins knew they would, as one of them—a "white warrior." Asking me to help him remove his tattoos signaled to me that Daniel was serious about disengaging. He still needed to do a great amount of work on his worldview and to rebuild his connection with society, but his willingness to cut his most visible ties to the ideology in such a physically permanent way meant it would be extremely difficult for him to go back even if he changed his mind. Removing them meant he was a "race traitor" to his former brothers. As a onetime Hammerskin leader myself, I knew how violently they would react if he tried to return.

After identifying the confusing feelings of dissatisfaction and self-hatred I had also experienced at his age, and after witnessing firsthand the violence at Charlottesville, Daniel couldn't square how he felt inside with what the movement forced him to become anymore. He knew something had to give. He just didn't know what—or how to make it happen in a way that didn't kill him.

He wanted to show the world not who he'd been but who he hoped to become. Daniel's visible tattoos were keeping him from potential jobs, relationships, and other outlets essential in building a more resilient, stable life. The same reason that extremists like Daniel made themselves so noticeable—to intimidate and strike fear—was now the same reason the tattoos were an obstacle for him. And, like many former extremists, they would cost thousands of dollars to remove, which Daniel didn't have. There was no erasing the violence he'd been involved in but removing his tattoos was a bold statement and a powerful milestone in divorcing himself from his beliefs.

When Daniel was ready to move forward with the removal, I called Buck, the timid but friendly owner of Lexington Tattoo Removal, located ninety minutes from where Daniel lived in Louisville. I had gotten to know Buck while working on a previous case, and he not only offered to remove Daniel's face tattoos for free, he also zapped the tattoos from his arms, chest, and hands. Buck became a friendly ear for Daniel over several months and a dozen brutally painful treatments.

I accompanied Daniel for his first session, wanting to be there for moral support and to show my gratitude to Buck in person for his generous and thoughtful gift. I warned Daniel it would sting a little. Having never done it myself (I've only had extensive tattoo coverups of all my old racist ink), I didn't know enough to tell the whole truth about how much it would actually hurt.

Daniel sat in a chair that resembled one from a new-age barbershop and closed his eyes. Buck kept a loud vacuum hose close to the laser tip to keep the smoke and smell of burned flesh from filling our nostrils but it wasn't loud enough to drown out the crackle and pop of rupturing ink molecules under charred layers of Daniel's skin. The first to go was the swastika covering his temple. "Jesus fucking Christ!" Daniel gasped.

It was far from over. As Buck began to erase the most noticeable of the tattoos over the next twenty minutes, each offered Daniel a new chance at liberating him from the vise that had gripped him for two years. The pain I felt watching Daniel was nowhere near what he endured. I give him credit for sticking it out through the burn of Buck's blue laser, wincing each time it erupted an inked spot on his skin.

"You were tough enough to get them put on, Daniel," I talked him through as he gritted his teeth, "you have to be tough enough to take them off."

Leveraging outside resources to assist in disengagement is critical.

I use every tool available to break down the remaining negative influences so the difficult process of helping an individual repair their potholes can begin. Tattoo removal provided Daniel a tangible, visible, and relatively quick way of showing me he was serious about disengagement. For others, the process is subtler. But in all cases, leveraging the power of resources and building new community around a person (that doesn't enable extremism) is necessary to give them the best opportunity to succeed in the long term. It's strength in numbers, and it bolsters the feeling of inclusion, if nothing else.

Daniel walked out of Buck's tattoo removal studio with a new lease on life, unbranded, though not free of his past indiscretions. We both knew this was only his first step in a long walk away from hate.

# 19

## The Quest for ICP

### Step Five: Lift
### *Reggie*

*Foster reintegration with humanity, while keeping aftercare lifelines open for ongoing support. A successful off-ramping means rebuilding personal and emotional resilience through healthy ICP replacement and positive interactions that work to replace demonization with humanization. Over time, repeated immersive experiences with willing, compassionate "others" can facilitate the examination of lingering ideological prejudices and reveal their fallacies.*

"I WANTED TO WALK UP BEHIND that goddamn raghead as he kissed the ground praying to unholy Muhammad," Reggie said, frequently pausing to take a drag from one of the menthol cigarettes he smoked incessantly. "And then kick him in his fucking *A-rab* throat. Kill that evil son of a bitch. Man, I would've done it, too...if I didn't have the dog and the baby with me."

"Reggie, are you sure it wasn't just someone doing yoga in the park?" I asked half joking. "Did you have a drink last night?" The second question wasn't in jest.

"Fuck no. Four years clean because of AA. Stone sober—no booze, no drugs." I could picture Reggie beaming with pride with this last response, along with an ashy Newport dangling from his lips. Even though he was angry as hell and pacing on the other end of the phone five hundred miles away in Buffalo, I learned after a handful of conversations to read his mood in the pattern of pulls on his cigarette.

"I'll be there tomorrow afternoon, Reggie," I said, trying to figure out a plan to assuage his sudden outburst of prejudice.

"Sounds good."

"Great."

"Do you like pizza?" Reggie asked.

I never hesitate to answer important questions. "New York pizza? Fuck no," I mocked. "Four years clean because of Chicago deep dish."

Reggie laughed. "Okay, guess I'll have plenty of delicious New York–style waiting for you, then."

Reggie's sarcasm meant he liked me.

Despite someone's genuine change of heart, no off-ramping is successful if they return from their rocky trek without gaining the proper insight to continue forward progress. One of the most powerful tools in my arsenal to supercharge an individual's disengagement is something I call an "immersion."

Immersions are interpersonal meetings where the subject and "others" come together in a safe and judgment-free environment to share the basis of each other's humanity. They are a lot like blind dates with willing opposites; a recovering Islamophobe meeting with an imam or a Muslim family; a Holocaust "skeptic" sitting in reflective conversation with a Holocaust survivor; a homophobe and a member of the LGBTQ community breaking bread over a home-cooked meal.

I am always present during these immersion sessions to facilitate safety first, respectful dialogue, and to guide the participants. I don't allow politics to be part of the discussion. Religion can be discussed only if it remains pluralistic and considerate.

The goal is to create cognitive dissonance in the people I work with and replace the demonization occurring in their minds with living, breathing humans, ultimately allowing them to reach their own conclusions about how their prejudice is unwarranted. I always prepare the incredible people who volunteer to be the "other" by communicating ground rules. They must be open-minded and brave, willing to hear upsetting words or ideas (though it rarely happens), and try to keep their composure as we correct misguided racist notions. Immersions are about seeding empathy where it may not exist and allowing space for honest teaching and learning. It's about breaking down barriers and filtering out noise to meet in the middle, not in a political or ideological sense but a shared and fundamentally human one.

It is easy to imagine that immersions aren't always perfect and are sometimes even difficult or prickly. Given the awkward and sometimes painful position it puts folks in, I never ask people in marginalized communities to take part if they are uncomfortable doing so. I also recognize it's not their responsibility—the victims of racism—to be nice to racists. Fortunately, I receive many requests from eager volunteers—of all faiths, ethnicities, and gender identities—who want to help me disengage extremists.

"Do you trust me, Reggie?"

We were driving through downtown Buffalo two hours after I landed at the airport and picked up my rental.

He sat in the passenger seat, staring out the side window, faded loose army fatigues and a black leather jacket hanging off his lanky frame. Reggie's face was more angular than it seemed in his Facebook profile picture, but his eyes were just as fierce. His pupils were like islands of cobalt floating in a sea of perpetually yellowed sadness, and his clothes reeked of cigarette smoke.

"Yeah," he paused. "I trust you. You ain't judged me once since we started talking three months ago. And you keep your word—you're here."

"Reggie, I need you to trust me—right now," I replied, slowing the Jeep as I pulled off the road to refuel.

"Why? You gonna make me eat sushi or some other Chink food?" He laughed, coughing sharply.

I stopped at the pump and shut off the ignition, suddenly aware that cutting off the engine meant the electronic doors would also unlock. I didn't think Reggie would run once I told him where we were headed, but I considered he might.

He saw the disappointment in my face and changed his demeanor once he recognized he said something racist. "I'm sorry, man. I didn't mean to say that."

"I need you to do something for me, Reggie."

"Sure, man. But you're kind of freaking me out." He grimaced. "You ain't gonna ask me to rob this gas station with you, are you? I've heard stories about you old Hammerskins." Whenever Reggie's twisted, deadpan humor came out of his mouth, it came with little warning.

"No!" I snorted. "Why the hell would you think I'd ask you to do that?"

With a straight face, he said, "I don't know. But I think you'd make a pretty badass stickup man if you ever wanted a career change."

"That's flattering, Reggie, thank you. No, what I need you to do takes more courage than armed robbery. I'm just not sure you're ready for it." I shrugged, patiently waiting for him to nibble on a morsel of reverse psychology. As I connected the gas nozzle to the Jeep, Reggie lit up a smoke and leaned up against the vehicle. "Forget it, who am I kidding? You're not ready for this. And put that cigarette out before you blow up my rental car and your ride home."

"You can't just bring it up and drop it. Now you gotta tell me. Don't leave me hanging, bro."

"All right, but I'm not sure you really have it in you yet, Reg," I teased as gently as I could.

"Brother, there ain't nothing I can't survive. Drugs, alcohol, boot camp, my dear old dad. Take your best shot. I'm ready."

Remembering the immediacy of the emotions he shared with me when he saw the Muslim man praying in the park, I knew Reggie needed a shock to his system.

"Have you ever met a Muslim person?" Not giving him time to reply, I continued, "Why do you think you wanted to hurt the Muslim guy who was just praying in the park?"

He shrugged. "Just hate them. Don't they seem sneaky to you behind those head covers and fancy robes? They make me nervous— like they're up to no good. And they hate America and freedom. And Jesus, well, they *really* hate Jesus."

"They're just regular people, Reggie. Like you, me, everybody else." I chose not to remind him that Catholics and the Klan were also partial to head coverings and robes.

"Yeah. Right."

We drove in silence for a few miles after filling up with gas. Sometimes silence with a captive audience is a very good thing. It provides time to reflect, but I didn't want Reggie to simmer too long. I couldn't afford to lose him now. "So, Reggie," I said as I maneuvered into a parking lot where we could finish the conversation without the distraction of the road. "Remember, you said you trusted me. I'm holding you to that."

It was with severe trepidation that Reggie exited my Jeep and followed behind me to the entrance of the mosque. I felt a tightening in my chest. Not because of where we were or how Reggie might react but because we were arriving late. I hoped our tardiness wouldn't detract from my respect and appreciation for the opportunity. Reggie took more effort to convince.

Riad was the imam of the Buffalo mosque who agreed to meet with us. I had stopped off to introduce myself for the first time on my way from the airport to Reggie's house that morning. Having Googled the mosque and Riad, I was confident the mosque's progressiveness—their website highlighted many pluralistic religious meet-ups—would be what Reggie needed.

I explained to Riad that Reggie was a Christian man—and a white supremacist. "I have to make a difficult request, Riad," I said. "I am friends with a man who I think could use your help. He has very strong prejudices against Islam—and Muslims." Riad grunted in recognition. "I am hoping we could stop by and speak with you later today. My friend doesn't know about this yet but I think it could help clarify his misunderstanding of Islam if he knew how similar your teachings are to his own. Would you mind if we dropped by for a chat?"

Riad paused, considering my heavy request. Then he agreed. "This man is of Allah, praise be unto him; he just doesn't know it. It would be my privilege."

I arranged to swing by a few hours later with Reggie—he knew nothing about it.

I rang the doorbell of the mosque when we arrived after hours. Reggie stood behind me with his hands stuffed into his pockets, his shoulders forward. He hadn't said a word to me since exiting the Jeep. I knew I had pissed him off and I was risking him feeling betrayed for not giving him forewarning about where I wanted to take him. I was counting on Reggie feeling different by the time we left the mosque.

Within seconds, the imam appeared at the door, stroking his salt-and-pepper beard. Riad wore a tan robe and brown wrap on his head. Reggie was nearly a full head taller than Riad but it didn't stop him from taking a defensive stance, although I doubted he even realized he'd done so.

"I'm sorry we're late, Riad."

His gentle face relaxed and he waved off my apologies. "Don't worry about it, my friend. But now I only have a few minutes to spare for you. I must prepare for a wedding celebration."

"Thank you. We'll take it," I said.

With a smile so warm it would have put anyone's qualms at ease, Riad gestured for us to remove our shoes at the door and follow him. Reggie shot me a quick, nervous glance. I smiled, and we stepped inside together. The mosque's interior was stunning, full of intricate murals and crescent moons painted throughout the sacred space, both peaceful and reverent. Riad led us down a hallway into the prayer hall. Reggie caught my side-eye, his head tipping toward the tall stained-glass windows lining one wall. The light that streamed through carried faint beams of pastel that painted the walls with color. The signs of faith were obvious. I could tell it impressed Reggie, though his nerves were obvious, too.

Quiet elegance filled the sanctuary. Beneath the arched windows rested simple furnishings. A mosaic pattern bordered the pristine white walls where they met the ceiling's edge. The few minutes Riad spared for us became two hours of us talking—and seeing one another as human beings. We sat on the red carpet in the center of the room talking about family and the values we hoped to pass down to our children. Riad discussed the Bible and the Quran, astonishing Reggie when he discovered Islamic teachings recognized Jesus as a prophet.

Riad and Reggie bonded over family and sports. And, of all the odd things to find common ground on, they made the greatest connection through martial arts film legend Chuck Norris. They were both huge fans of his movies. As they say, Chuck Norris *can* do anything, I suppose. I witnessed the changing of a dark heart that, not long before this meeting, felt disdain for a Muslim man for praying in the park.

Reggie lacked healthy community. When that's true, and available resources to help someone are scarce, the help of others—everyday citizens in *lifting* them can prove immense. While I never asked Riad to do it, he was proactively filling Reggie's ICP deficits.

As we sat in the open sanctuary, I felt the intentions of all who had prayed there—the same hopes we all share. We want happiness. We want security for our families. We want them to have solid educations, good health, and to receive an opportunity to lead fulfilling lives. All of us need to feel seen, we crave a sense of agency, and we all want to be part of something that contributes to the greater good.

But none of us get a free ride for our mistakes—the road to redemption should not be easy. We all encounter obstacles in life, and we all experience the pain of love and loss, but despite that, only some of us make the choice to be hateful and violent. Simply erasing our poor decisions isn't enough. As it should be, disengagement is hard work. But recovery must also be allowed to start somewhere, and realistic expectations—especially the time line—must be clear. Nothing happens overnight. Likewise, immersions aren't like waving a magic wand. Expect that repeated immersion sessions may be required before seeing results. It's also important to encourage ongoing exposure to a variety of diverse groups for long-term change to occur.

Reggie and Riad bonded over their common struggles and joys, recognizing everyone alive is battling invisible demons. That we are all human, we can all love, and we're all capable of accepting love—if we allow ourselves to.

After Reggie and I left the mosque, he was beaming. He didn't say much, but what I saw wash over him was something I sensed he hadn't felt in a long time, or ever. It looked like clarity. Like he found an answer to something after searching in the muck and grime of hate for years. After a lifetime of darkness, a pinpoint of light had penetrated.

"Do you think I'll like hummus?" Reggie asked me in the car as I drove him home from the mosque.

In the smiling selfie that Reggie sent me of himself and Riad eating lunch at the local falafel stand the following week, it appeared he did.

# 20

## Building Bridges

### Step Six: Love
#### *Daniel*

*A post-extremist life requires ongoing social support rooted in positive and life-affirming experiences, resilience-building, and the healthy fulfillment of ICP. During this step, ensure individuals are surrounded by a community that can help them focus on self-reflection and cautious vulnerability.*

ONE OF THE MOST PROFOUND experiences I have ever witnessed is Daniel's meeting with Susan Bro, whose daughter is Heather Heyer, the young woman who was murdered at the Charlottesville rally.

I felt an instant connection with Susan the first time we met. Sweet but blunt, with silvery-gray hair and square glasses at the tip of her nose, we were strangers for only a moment. Her warm heart and wise words exuded kindness from the time she embraced me in her arms. Accepting me, a former Nazi, into her home to discuss the raw and painful emotions still fresh from her daughter's death only four months prior was one of the most courageous things I have ever witnessed.

After Daniel's mom, Janet, told me he attended the Unite the Right rally, I felt disheartened, to say the least. I thought he was in a better place. Daniel broke away from the ideology after the rally but had not broken from the actual people—they were like family for him. He hadn't found his way completely out of the wilderness and there was nothing waiting on the other side to keep him from going back.

I asked Susan if she would consider meeting Daniel. I knew the request was a difficult one. It meant facing Heather's death—again—and engaging with a white supremacist who attended the rally, while her family was still facing harassment from neo-Nazis who blamed her innocent daughter for their despicable acts. It was heavy, and I felt its full weight.

Susan did, too. But after a long, silent pause, she said yes. She would meet with Daniel because she knew her daughter would have done it. She took out her phone and showed me a video that Heather's friend posted the day of the rally that proved her point. In it, Heather attempts a civil conversation with an alt-right woman at the rally thirty minutes before a marcher ran Heather down with his car and killed her. Susan hoped neither her daughter's life nor her death was in vain, though she also recognized the issue went far beyond Heather—the death of her white daughter shouldn't overshadow centuries of tragedies endured by people of color. Susan decided that if meeting Daniel could help stop someone—anyone—from acting out of hate, it was worth pursuing. While Susan's compassion awes me, it must be said: it is *never* the responsibility of the victim, a person of color, or anyone harmed by racism or hate to feel they must extend themselves to those who have hurt them, though it's also fair to consider that most victimizers also began their journeys as victims. The cycle must end somewhere.

Now, I just had to convince Daniel to meet Susan.

As expected, our conversation was complicated.

"She won't blame you for something you didn't do, Daniel," I tried assuaging his biggest fear. "But I won't fault her if she holds us both accountable. Everything we do has consequences, good or bad. Sometimes, the results of our poor choices fester and don't emerge until long after we've figured out there's a better way of doing things."

That was a realization I had spent many years meditating on.

Susan and Daniel met in an empty church outside of Charlottesville the following week, and it was one of the most humbling moments I have ever witnessed. Light shone through the stained-glass windows with tinted beams that vibrated and echoed inside the vacancy of the holy space. The worn, wooden pews reminded me of those from the chapel of my Catholic grade school, long before I'd known anything about skinheads or Nazis or Charlottesville's history of slavery. In my memory, I pictured bald Monsignor O'Leary in front of the altar with his arms wide, reciting a psalm, and singing "Hallelujah" off-key. But there was no Catholic school priest here now; no altar boys smelling of incense and sacramental wine; no snoring, hungover, elderly Italian men being nudged by their wives in the back row. Only one lost young man ready to find his way home—and a confoundingly brave mother ready to help him.

Susan extended her hand to Daniel when I introduced them. He was nervous, approaching with his arms crossed and his hands tucked under his armpits. After a pause, his feet planted, he loosened up and gently accepted her palm in his. I took a seat in the pew next to Susan and broke the awkward silence to ask about Heather. Susan spoke of her daughter's idealistic, kind, and inclusive demeanor, but she also included the hardships Heather faced growing up. After letting it sink in, I asked Daniel to share his own upbringing with Susan, after which she pointed out that he and Heather had suffered many of the same challenges in life. It surprised Daniel to know how much Heather's experience resembled his own. Both had hardscrabble upbringings in broken homes where addiction was generational. For Daniel, both his mom and dad had abused drugs and alcohol. For Heather, her estranged father was the addict.

I could see how Susan's revelation shocked Daniel's system. He'd gone to the rally just four months earlier and stood with his white-supremacist tribe against people who were there to oppose them—one of whom was Heather Heyer. After hearing of Heather's death, Daniel got caught up in movement propaganda that called her a "cultural Marxist"—a common trope from the far-right that paints the opposition as "socialist" agitators allegedly paid by powerful provocateurs like billionaire philanthropist (and demonized Jewish figure) George Soros—though Daniel later learned through a lighthearted rebuke from Susan that the characterization couldn't have been more untrue. He never expected to have anything in common with Heather or Susan. I sensed his shame again through his downward stare and slumped shoulders as he became certain that other conspiracy theories had also duped him over the years.

Susan shared with Daniel how much she loved her daughter and the overwhelming sorrow she felt in the hospital when the police officer informed her that Heather died. Daniel lowered himself onto the church pew. I fought back tears as I held Susan's hand, having just witnessed two people from disparate worlds find a connection point through one another's pain and sorrow. For Susan to look beyond her heartbreak into Daniel's eyes, past his faded Nazi tattoos, with unconditional forgiveness was remarkable. As their conversation ended, Susan turned to Daniel and said, "I'm sorry someone manipulated you."

Daniel paused. "I am sorry you lost Heather."

They both rose, and Susan asked Daniel if she could hug him.

Daniel hesitated for a long time, swaying his torso like a pendulum, his lips pulled together in a tight line and eyes brimming with uncertainty. They darted to me for an answer, but my eyes were too busy smiling. I recognized the recoil of his body, though. It meant he was bracing for punishment. Daniel didn't know what a hug felt like. Years of abuse had conditioned him to confuse affection as the first sign of attack. I nodded my head in support. Daniel took a step toward Susan and opened his arms wide as they walked into each other's embrace.

The selfless compassion that Susan showed made an indelible impression on me—and Daniel, too. The impact of the encounter left us all hopeful that hate could indeed be broken.

# 21

---

## Free Radical

### Step Seven: Live
### *Kassandra*

*We delight in the beauty of the butterfly, but rarely admit the changes it has gone through to achieve that beauty.*

—Maya Angelou

P LEASE TELL ME WHERE YOU ARE," Meredith begged Kassandra when she finally called from a pay phone forty-eight hours after she went missing. "I'll bring you what you've asked for but I need to hand it to you in person, to see for myself you're all right." Meredith regained her composure, tears flowing down her cheeks. To bring Kassandra home, she could not let her emotions or fear get the best of her.

"Are you with Jakob now, honey?" Meredith could barely separate his name from the sting it left on her lips.

"Yes, Mother. We're just outside of California," Kassandra replied. "We're planning to get married soon, I guess."

Meredith shut her eyes and swallowed the thought, clearing her throat. "All the more reason I should bring you both some money to live on—and whatever else you need, in person. I want to meet my future son-in-law first before you do that, Kassandra. It's tradition. Your father does, too."

"No!" Kassandra shouted. "Not Dad." Meredith pulled the phone from her ear. She took in a deep breath.

*Please deposit more money to continue your call.*

"Okay, honey. Okay. I understand. Until you're ready, your father will stay home. But please—"

"Fine!" Kassandra screamed. "Just you, then. We're out of money, and I have to go." She restated her demands and said she'd call again later that evening to arrange logistics to meet in the following days.

After Meredith hung up, she booked a flight to meet up with me in San Francisco, then called me to play a recording of the exchange with her daughter. I noticed things in the conversation right away that made me nervous. For instance, Kassandra wavered after stating they would marry, saying, "We're planning to get married soon, *I guess*." Was it a clue from a naïve girl, once awed by the romantic overtures of a stranger, now realizing the danger she was in after meeting him in person? My intuition said it was doubt—which also meant a window of hope. But I feared Kassandra was becoming desensitized to her new circumstances. Her positive feelings toward her captor and her negativity, such as her continued anger and distrust of her parents and me, told me she was being manipulated. Her tone was hard to decipher, but she sounded tired, tenuous. Like she wanted to be alone and back in her bedroom. My gut told me her captor had coached her on the responses and role-played scenarios with her. While I never detected fear that could have signaled an immediate crisis, there was hesitancy and a very different tone of uncertainty in Kassandra's voice. Like a kid suddenly realizing they were lost inside a shopping mall.

After my probing in Union City failed to turn up any leads beyond an address, Kassandra surprised Meredith with a truck-stop phone call to ask for cash, her Social Security card, and her passport. While it was great to know she was alive, we knew she might use those items to leave the country with her abductor, so we pivoted our approach, unsure of what to expect. Meredith told Kassandra she would deliver the items she'd asked for, but to buy time, she said she misplaced the passport and needed time to track it down. When Kassandra's follow-up call came, Meredith played it like a pro. She hatched a plan to meet Kassandra in person forty-eight hours later.

Across the street from the restaurant where Meredith was inside waiting to meet Kassandra, I slouched in the driver's seat of my rental Jeep like a crack detective in a film noir. From the cocked rearview mirror, I spied the real Jakob Bergsson for the first time—at least the one on US soil. A blizzard of ideas had stormed through my head as to what the people behind the Bergsson alias looked like, but none of them included a dark-skinned Latino man. Santiago Amaro—as I now knew his name to be—was driving toward me with Kassandra from the opposite end of the block in his white Mercedes.

I sunk lower to avoid detection, hoping the plan hadn't already gone sideways and endangered Kassandra.

After his car was no longer visible to me from my perch beneath the steering wheel, I risked inching up higher in my seat to get a full view of the block. Brake lights lit up on a car several hundred feet ahead of me. I watched in horror as the Mercedes shifted into reverse gear and backed up toward me. Fifty feet before reaching my Jeep, it lurched forward and swung a U-turn before darting toward me again. *Had he seen me? Did I alert Kassandra?*

If they spotted me now and blew my cover so close to intercepting Kassandra, I would never forgive myself. Heart pounding, I sat up straight, leaned into the steering wheel, and watched in my rearview as the white Mercedes drove down the block and made a sharp, right-hand turn away from the meeting point.

*This can't be happening. He knows the location, and there are plenty of open parking spots in the lot.* We were careful and deliberate. The plan was solid. My Jeep couldn't have tipped him off. I messaged the private investigator already inside the restaurant. Meredith was also inside seated at a booth, visible to the detective sitting discreetly across the busy diner. We rehearsed it in our heads several times—there hadn't been enough time for a physical run-through. Had Meredith appeared too nervous and telegraphed the setup?

I was certain she hadn't. Meredith was convincing when she told Kassandra she would bring her the money and passport with one condition—that, in her words, she "meet Jakob in person."

"He won't agree to that," Kassandra had fired back without missing a beat.

"Sweetie, we just want to make sure you're safe. Your father and I want you to have some money to survive. I know you have none right now. We don't want you to worry about where you'll sleep and how to pay for food. You say you will marry him—Jakob. I'm sure you understand, that as your mother, why I need…why I would like to meet the young man my daughter will marry, the future father of my grandkids."

When the call came from Kassandra to tell Meredith that Jakob agreed to meet with her, it was the first time Meredith smiled in eighteen months. But now, hope just drove away with her daughter around the corner in a late-model, white Mercedes-Benz.

As I slid my key into the ignition to follow them, the car reappeared. It was drifting toward me, so I flung my seat backward. Adrenaline flowing, I prayed he wouldn't slow down again or park on the street nearby. If either of them recognized me, it was over.

From my awkward vantage point, I watched upside down through the rearview mirror as he pulled up beside me on the street. The squeal of wasted brake pads told me he stopped, so close I could hear his radio through both of our rolled-up windows. Kassandra was probably inches away from me in the passenger seat, though I couldn't risk looking. I held my breath, contemplating my options for the shifting scenario.

*Do they see me? Should I jump out and grab her now?*

Relief washed over me when the diminishing sound of metallic friction told me he'd pulled away slowly. Poking my head up like a contorted gopher, I saw enough to see the Mercedes pull into an open spot in the restaurant's parking lot. I shot our undercover flatfoot a text: *They just parked. Very close call. Be ready.*

Jack and Meredith chose a female private investigator to avoid suspicion, but also because they were hoping Kassandra might respond better to a woman if there was a need to physically intervene. She'd sent photos of the diner's layout the day before the meeting to strategize an exit plan. I couldn't risk anyone seeing me in case there were other eyes on the place, so we chose a booth close to the front door for Meredith, while the investigator sat opposite the entryway with a clear view of where they would be sitting. She kept me apprised of everything that happened once Kassandra and Amaro entered. When the detective texted me back to report they had sat down in the booth across from Meredith, I climbed out of the Jeep to stretch my cramped back, knowing I might have to move quickly if things got tense.

Making my way across the cracked sidewalk into the parking lot, I was careful not to draw attention to myself. Amaro parked his white Mercedes in a spot away from the front of the restaurant, shielded by a van that looked like it hadn't moved in years.

I checked as best I could for anyone in my vicinity—an accomplice— a spotter, perhaps. Seeing no one, I kneeled next to the front tire of his car, wedged a twig inside his valve cap, and released the air from it. In the unlikely event Amaro got past me with Kassandra in the diner, this was cheap insurance they wouldn't get far.

A silent text vibrated my phone as the tire let out its final gasp.

*Menus just arrived. They're ordering coffee and just talking.* It was now or never. This was our best chance to intervene and divert Kassandra from her captor. Not my typical extremist disengagement scenario, but it seemed no better options existed, and if Amaro got away with Kassandra, we might never see her again.

Nervous small-talk from Meredith would keep them distracted long enough for me to move in unnoticed.

I pulled open the glass door of the diner and entered with my head down, cap pulled low, and picked up the pace once I closed in on them. Just as Amaro's eyes lifted from his menu, I slid my body into the booth against his, wedging him between me and Kassandra, who was pressed up against the wall. Only Meredith, seated across from us—and the investigator the family hired stationed twenty yards away—knew what was happening. I swept the utensils on the table out of Amaro's reach and turned to him.

I tried to lock onto his dodging eyes.

Santiago Amaro, the Peruvian American who was half of the elusive "Jakob Bergsson," was a man in his midthirties who lived, presumably, with his mother and sister in Union City, California. He was dark-skinned and short—not much more than five feet and change—and had a wandering hazel eye and a stable dark brown one buried under a deep brow. The puffy, royal-blue waterproof windbreaker he wore, like the cold-weather ones that roll up into a small sack, looked pockmarked with cigarette burn holes. Amaro was far from handsome, and I wondered how Kassandra must have felt when she realized that "Jakob Bergsson" was not what she envisioned. It seemed she hadn't come to grips with the contradiction yet, even after the "Jakob" who picked her up at school was the opposite of the Aryan super boy from his stolen photos and videos.

Kassandra caught me with her shiny, sleep-deprived eyes, exhaustion surrounding them with rings of black. That's when anger hit me. It radiated in ripples through my skin and in my bones, reminding me of what I hated about myself a lifetime ago. I shook off the unwelcome feeling and loosened my fists, as bitter contempt for Amaro ran through me for what he had dumped on Kassandra and her family. I pitied his miserable existence.

Boxed in by a wall of windows on one side and a nervous Peruvian with an angry white man practically sitting on him on the other, Kassandra rose and leaned forward over the table. She looked at me and, without her usual hesitation, said, "Christian, don't. He loves me."

Amaro yanked Kassandra back down as she pleaded with me through emotionless words as she recoiled to avoid his tightening grip.

He grabbed her arm again with force. Helpless, she turned to Meredith. "Jakob wants to marry me. He wants to have babies with me."

Eyes glued to her daughter, Meredith said nothing.

*This was taking too long.* "We know who you are, Santiago Amaro, and what you're doing to Kassandra and the other girls," I said.

Just like that, he snapped into his online Jakob Bergsson persona—German accent and all. Every trace of his nervousness evaporated, and he became the hard-boiled Nazi I'd hunted—the snarly racist who would not let a "kike-loving cuck" like me interfere with his plans for Kassandra. He lunged across the table for the knife that rested in front of Meredith, grabbing it with remarkable speed.

A step faster than remarkable, I wrestled it from his grip. Clutching the thin piece of steel in one hand, I found my other forearm instinctively pressed against Nazi Jakob's windpipe. After flipping the sweaty knife from my balled fist toward Meredith, I removed the pressure from against his throat.

The restaurant manager hurried over; his lily-white face drained of color. Whispering too politely given the circumstances, he asked if everything was all right, and I sensed that he thought I was the problem. My full-body tattoos and the scowl on my face might have anyone arrive at that guess. Other customers stopped their chatter to stare in our direction.

"Is everything *all right?*" I whispered back, getting louder with each statement, while keeping my focus on Amaro. "This man trades explicit photos with underage girls, then stalks and lures them across state lines. So, no, we're not all right. I think you should call the police." I meant it to be more of a threat than request, hoping it might spook Amaro to slip up.

We had put the local police on notice about the situation earlier that morning, though they claimed they could not intervene because Kassandra turned eighteen two weeks before she went missing. They would assist if we needed backup, they assured us, warning us in the same breath not to break any local ordinances.

"It's time for you to take a walk with your mom, Kassandra. Take a breather, talk to her," I said. "When I get up, I want you to slide out of the booth over Jakob and go with her. We don't want this to get ugly in here."

"Stay where you are," Amaro snarled at her, pulling her again by the wrist toward him.

Kassandra looked around at each of us, lost. Meredith kept her cool as her daughter fell back against her abductor.

"I'm staying with Jakob," she said.

"Please, honey, come with me for just a little while. Christian will stay with Jakob and work everything out."

"Listen to her, Kassandra," I pleaded. "Go with your mom. We can't do this here. They'll have us all arrested—and Jakob will get deported." I rolled the dice, the irony of the threat not lost on me.

The mention of deportation brought fear to his eyes for the first time.

The threat made Amaro paranoid and wily. I took advantage of his sudden confusion and flipped my approach. "If you still want to stay with Jakob after hearing what your mom wants to say, I will bring him to you."

I hated lying, but it was the only way to separate them at that moment. Kassandra was not thinking clearly. Even though I had exposed the massive web of lies spun by Jakob Bergsson, she still seemed to want to be with this peculiar stranger named Santiago Amaro, who took advantage of her and had lied to her for eighteen months. Meredith was ready to take her daughter and head straight to the airport. And there was no way I would let Amaro move an inch until she was in Meredith's car and safely on her way home to New Jersey.

Kassandra rose slowly from her seat, tears in her eyes. I released the force of my body against Amaro's and swung my legs out of the booth for her thin frame to squeeze past us. Reminding myself that my wife would take serious issue with me getting locked up in a California jail for aggravated battery, I kept my arms tucked at my sides and braced myself for any of Amaro's wayward blows.

Before leaving the restaurant with Meredith, Kassandra turned and offered her Jakob a pitiful goodbye. It was a final farewell. The investigator signaled me via text once they were in the car and out of sight. I shifted from my seat and stood, slowly releasing Amaro from solitary confinement. He followed my lead and got up carefully. I dropped some bills onto the table for the coffees and to compensate the manager for the disruption I caused, then led Amaro out without fuss to minimize drawing any more attention.

"Here's what happens now," I told him once we were outside, my face inches from his. "We're going back to your place to get Kassandra's things. I already know where you live, and I assume you do, too. You'd be smart to meet me there in ten minutes."

"Why the fuck would I do that?" he shot back, his voice deeper and sounding more German than before—a trait he shared with his Russian counterpart.

"The police are already there and starting an investigation, so either you bring me her things, or they will go in to find them."

As he walked toward his Mercedes in the parking lot while I followed behind, he noticed the flat tire on his car.

"*Motherf—*"

"Today isn't your day. Ten minutes. See you there."

"I can't drive on a flat. It'll ruin my rim."

"Shoot," I said, "you're right. You can ride with me if you want."

He yanked his car door open and opted to slide into his own driver's seat.

Before pulling away in my Jeep, I dialed the private investigator to confirm she'd gotten word to the cops that Kassandra was safe and with her mom.

"I'm heading to the house now. It may be a while, Amaro's having... car issues, but he could still give us trouble when he rolls up. Remind the cops that Kassandra is on the missing persons' list if they push back. Because she's eighteen now, they'll try to dismiss it as a lovers' spat."

I arrived a few minutes later and waited for Amaro to grind along on his bare rim. We were impossible to miss across the street from his house, me and the half dozen cops wearing Kevlar vests. Hands resting on their weapons and radios squawking with chatter, they looked intimidating. And I was ready.

After twenty minutes, the Mercedes pulled into the driveway. Amaro sat inside his car with the ignition running, refusing to get out or move. So, we waited. One minute. Two. Five. Seven. All I cared about was seeing him arrested for sharing pornography with an underage girl and helping fleece a nation with a hostile foreign partner—but I also wanted to retrieve Kassandra's belongings so I could deliver them to her and Meredith at the airport. The cops were there only to retrieve lost property and wrap up an abduction call; they weren't even aware of Amaro's involvement with dark-web pornography, online drug sales, and Russian trolls, even though the hired investigator had briefed their sergeant that morning with all the lurid details. I didn't have the time or the patience to take them down that winding path right now. Kassandra was safe with her mom, but her beloved violin and her computer, with sensitive log-in information, were not.

Amaro continued to sit inside his Mercedes for an additional thirty minutes while I dished out relevant CliffsNotes on the case to the cops. I couldn't guess what Amaro was thinking. None of us could, and it made us nervous. Was he going to come out shooting? Turn a gun on himself and pull the trigger? Suicide by cop? I wasn't sure if he had a weapon in the car, though my cursory peek through his window in the parking lot didn't raise any flags.

Speaking through a loudspeaker, the lead police officer on-site directed him to exit his vehicle and come over to talk to them.

He ignored the invitation.

The officer gave the direction again, wasting his breath. Amaro neither responded nor budged. When I pushed for quicker resolution, the lead cop informed me that since he had violated no law—Kassandra was over eighteen and no longer a missing person—there was nothing they could do to force him to comply. It was his driveway and his car. He wasn't a criminal in their eyes, just a nuisance with a troubled love life. Apparently, I was wasting their time.

"Her things are in the house," I reminded them.

"She would have to file a complaint," said the lieutenant.

I worried the police would leave soon, whether he got out of the car or not. From his vantage point, I suspected Amaro had similar thoughts about stalling. So, I pressed the lieutenant and asked if I could approach Amaro's vehicle.

He didn't have a reason for stopping me but cautioned it wasn't a good idea and advised me not to break any laws or I'd be arrested.

Before the cop could finish his warning, I turned and walked across the street and up the driveway to the car and rapped my knuckle on the driver's-side window.

"Open the door, Santiago. Step out of the vehicle."

I spooked him as he texted on his phone. I hoped he wouldn't realize I had zero authority to force him out of his car. Leveraging the visible police presence behind me, I knew the optics were in my favor. But I was running out of time.

"This doesn't have to be worse than it already is. Do you see those police officers over there? I'm going in with them now to get Kassandra's things." I was out of earshot of the cops across the street being kept preoccupied by our private eye, so I pressed him at a stern hush.

This got Amaro's attention. He cracked open his window. "No, stay here," he said. "I'll get her things and bring them out."

I didn't know exactly what things he was referring to. All I knew was that Kassandra's laptop contained sensitive personal and family information, and he had her beloved violin. Deciding not to press my luck, I stepped back, my palm on his car door to give him limited space to exit his vehicle. As he squeezed out, he made a speed-walk attempt for the front door of the house. I followed a step behind, stopping when we reached the entrance to his home, looking for any legal reason to rush in after him.

"Keep the door open. You have sixty seconds before me and all these cops follow you in," I upped the ante with another bluff. It scared him enough to cooperate, but I couldn't risk him changing his mind or making any impulsive moves. I also knew that if too much time passed—or he called my bluff—I'd leave empty-handed. Kassandra needed her violin for closure. It was the only thing that quelled her anxiety. Getting the computer back was a precaution; we didn't want it anywhere near him, fearing what information he might find in it to further exploit the family.

Amaro disappeared into the house, leaving the door ajar. Brushing it open wider with my foot, I could sense the cops' tension over my actions from where I stood. We were all thinking the same thing—how long it would be before I rushed in after him. I reminded myself I only survived my tenuous past because in the end I somehow always kept a cool head. This time felt different. I was overheating with thoughts of revenge. It took every ounce of restraint to not go in after him, lock the door behind me, and take care of business before the cops could rush in.

Just then, Amaro appeared in front of me. He tossed out only one item—Kassandra's violin case—and slammed the door. The deadbolt I had flipped on the doorjamb while he went inside brought the heavy wooden door bouncing back toward his face, knocking straight back into his chin, and dazing him.

"Where's the rest?" I asked, knowing I was pushing my luck. Part of me didn't want to give him another chance to go back in to regroup. I was his bitter nemesis, the man who'd hunted Jakob Bergsson to expose his lies, his connections, and revealed his scheme to Kassandra. With his Russian counterpart, Amaro had coordinated a bitter troll attack on me and my family for over a year.

"That's all of it," he snapped, rubbing his jaw. Nervous about me entering, he reached to disengage the lock.

I wanted to grab him by the throat and throttle him for the damage he caused to a vulnerable teen and her family—and mine.

"Stay away from Kassandra and everyone she knows," I said. "Disappear. This is your only warning."

Santiago Amaro stepped back, turned away from me, and let the door shut behind him as I stood on the other side of it holding Kassandra's violin case.

Police found no grounds to investigate him further; Kassandra was of age, and I had recovered her property to her satisfaction. The case was closed in their eyes. Though, as I saw it, not a damn thing changed. I knew Amaro would strike again. Maybe not with Kassandra, she was only one fish in a massive barrel and he and his reckless cohort had an endless supply of scatter-shot ammunition to hunt with.

I hurried to meet up with Meredith and Kassandra where they waited for me at the tram stop inside the San Francisco airport. Kassandra avoided my eyes as I walked up but reached out her hand for the violin and thanked me for returning it to her. It was a relief to know that something other than Jakob Bergsson and the alt-right was still important to her. Standing behind her, with arms wrapped around her daughter's thin frame, Meredith mouthed *thank you* to me. Tears welled in her eyes. After we parted ways, I cried, too.

Meredith later told me what she could without breaking Kassandra's confidence about what happened during her time with Amaro. It was not the storybook tale Kassandra hoped for. Too steeped in fantasy to recognize that her first-ever boyfriend wasn't who he claimed, she gave in and resigned herself to go along with Amaro's wishes—who stayed in character as the Nazi Jakob Bergsson the entire time.

On the first day, he charmed Kassandra with poetry and roadside flowers. By the next, Amaro became impatient and controlling. He chose where they ate, ordering without considering what Kassandra might want. When they stopped to sleep was his choice alone, as were the television programs they watched in the seedy motel rooms he chose to nap in. Amaro didn't allow Kassandra out of his sight and had no interest in hearing her out—especially when it came to ideology. He was the authority on National Socialism, not Kassandra. Amaro became dismissive of her within the first few hours, abrupt, and showed "affection"—though it was sexual assault—as he forced himself on Kassandra against her wishes. She later claimed she didn't see it as abuse, though it was. She saw it as her duty to succumb to him—for the "privilege" of making Bergsson Nazi babies.

Though I never saw Santiago Amaro again—or heard anything more from the likes of "Jakob Bergsson"—endless iterations of Internet soldiers have continued to harass me. I've learned to quarantine the attacks and memories, so damage is never more than nominal. In the end, even "Santiago Amaro" turned out to be an alias, and the family in Union City moved. My continued efforts to find someone to bring these people to justice and warn the other victims never materialized. I'm terrified knowing that someone who still lives freely in America is conspiring with a foreign enemy to bait everyday Americans, a man who went rogue for the sexual assault of a young girl still roams free.

What became of the Russian, Maksim Volkov, the other half of the Bergsson alias, and any other anonymous accomplices—or the thousands of foreign cyber trolls that still plague the "free" Internet and continue to destabilize our democracy—remains an unsatisfying conclusion for me. In the years since the 2016 election, we've learned that Vladimir Putin's network of Internet troll farms and their nefarious social media tactics exceeded my worst imaginings, and we still don't know the full scope of their efforts. Only with time will we be able to assess the breadth of damage caused by Russia's ongoing code war against Western democracies like the United States.

One thing that's grown increasingly clear, is the human cost of law enforcement's failure to recognize the global threat posed by white supremacy. Had the information I passed along to the FBI about Russia's meddling before the presidential election in November 2016 concerned brown-skinned Islamist extremists, I have no doubt the intelligence would have been acted on. But in those last weeks of Obama's presidency—or since—it seemed nothing was done about it.

Former Trump national security advisors Katharine Gorka and her husband, Sebastian Gorka, immediately acted to downplay, if not eliminate, domestic white-supremacist extremism as a national security focus and terror threat.* The Trump administration bet the house on "radical Islam." A month later, white nationalists marched in Charlottesville, leaving behind their own trail of blood. Three years later, a white nationalist opened fire in a Walmart store in El Paso, Texas, killing twenty-two Mexican Americans and inspiring a string of copycats in the weeks after. In what's called *stochastic terrorism*—or randomized acts of targeted violence inspired by the fear rhetoric of ideologues—before the El Paso attack, the shooter allegedly posted a "manifesto" online containing racist, anti-immigrant language and ideas that some argue directly echoed President Trump's language regarding an "invasion" by Latin American immigrants.

Meanwhile, as federal authorities scramble to understand the threat of domestic extremism to keep Americans safe, the stream of hate flowing from the rusty, old bigot spigot continues—as does the endless work of breaking it:

*We met last night at your lecture at the Museum of Tolerance in Los Angeles. Your work moved me but I about fell out of my chair when you shared Kassandra's story. Her exact scenario happened to my niece. While her parents were able to intercept her at the airport, we're worried she's still in touch with her "twenty-year-old Nazi beau." I imagine you're busy these days but we don't know what to do. Would you be open to a phone call? Thank you very much.*

—Douglas

*Douglas, I think I can help. What's your phone number?*

—Christian

---

* Eli Stokols, Bryan Bender, and Michael Crowley, "The Husband and Wife Team Driving Trump's National Security Policy," *Politico*, accessed August 8, 2019, https://www.politico.com/story/2017/02/trump-national-security-gorka-234950/.

# 22

## TBD (To Be De-Radicalized)

### *Richard*

T. S. ELIOT WROTE, "APRIL IS THE CRUELEST MONTH." And every year since I denounced white supremacy in 1996, the days that surround April 20 have spooked me. Marked by the blood of innocent victims of extremist violence throughout our American history, it's also a day celebrated by neo-Nazis worldwide to honor the birth of Adolf Hitler.

On April 19, 1993, US federal agents stormed the Branch Davidian complex in Waco, Texas, following a fifty-one-day armed standoff with cult leader David Koresh and his followers. The botched raid resulted in the deaths of seventy-six members of the religious cult, including women and children. Federal agents killed Koresh but also lost four of their own.

On the same day in April, eight years before the Waco incident, federal agents raided the compound of another cult, this one belonging to a militant white-supremacist group—the Covenant, the Sword, and the Arm of the Lord (CSA)—which resulted in a four-day armed standoff.

On April 19, 1995, survivalist militia member and Aryan Nations sympathizer Timothy McVeigh—inspired by the racist Christian Identity teachings of CSA—detonated a truck bomb in Oklahoma City that killed 168 men, women, and children.

For anti-government militias, the middle of April is also significant because it was the start of the American Revolution, a bloody culture war they believe will bloom again.

In Denver, on April 20, 1999, two masked students wearing black trench coats entered Columbine High School and opened fire, massacring thirteen of their classmates before turning the guns on themselves.

On April 15, 2013, the Tsarnaev brothers launched a deadly ISIS-inspired terror attack during the Boston Marathon, which left three people dead and hundreds more injured.

Although I acknowledge it's plausible that the timings of these events are pure coincidence, I still get anxious when the April storms appear on the horizon. So, when I arrived in Whitefish, Montana, on April 20, 2017—Hitler's birthday—I was on my toes.

It was here where I came face-to-face with Richard Spencer, the alt-right agitator best known as the fair-haired white nationalist in the smart Brooks Brothers suit and tie who was sucker punched by an anti-fascist counterprotester during a live news broadcast outside of Donald Trump's presidential inauguration ceremony. And while my initial contact to help a white supremacist leave the movement usually comes from a person who wants to get out, or from one of their loved ones, I do not forgo any opportunity to engage with extremists—especially if I think I can establish rapport as a first step toward moving beyond hate. Entrenched in the alt-right movement, Richard had just unleashed a panic on his hometown of Whitefish when I met him.

The Montana Human Rights Network (MHRN) invited me to address the local Whitefish community four months after suffering a vicious Nazi "troll storm"—a barrage of targeted harassment and threats. The catalyst for the December troll storm was a commercial property dispute between Spencer's mother and a local Whitefish Realtor, a Jewish woman. The MHRN was working with victims of the attack and thought I could help shed light on what they were up against.

In Richard, they were up against a white nationalist with a fanatical following. Before he was famously punched outside the inauguration ceremony, Richard was best known for a different viral video captured by the media just after the 2016 election.

"Hail Trump!" Spencer shouted in the video to an audience of over two hundred during his private rally in Washington, DC, to honor the new president-elect. Standing onstage, he raised his glass and toasted, "Hail our people! Hail victory!" Spencer's enthusiasm elicited loud cheers and Nazi salutes from the crowd, an image that forced the nation to pay close attention.

Spencer proceeded that night to refer to the mainstream media in attendance as the *lügenpresse,* or "lying press," a term used by the Third Reich throughout the Second World War to discredit their critics, as Trump has done with the misappropriation of the term *fake news.* Spencer then called for a "peaceful ethnic cleansing of America," prompting more Nazi salutes from the audience.

The notoriety that Richard Spencer brought to his hometown was far from welcome. A onetime railroad hub, by the 1940s Whitefish had developed into a cozy and quiet upscale ski village of fewer than seven thousand inhabitants—mostly seasonal ski bums and bunnies who only visited when the Rocky Mountain powder was fresh—the Flathead Valley community savored small comforts, like their beloved Huckleberry Days Arts Festival. Townspeople enjoyed lazy Sundays reading the local *Flathead Beacon* newspaper. They were not accustomed to scathing *Washington Post* headlines painting Whitefish as the home of America's most influential racist. Many who lived there were longtime residents who'd known the Spencer family, but few knew of Richard's dangerous rhetoric or his rising alt-right movement.

In response to the attention, a group of residents considered voicing their concern to Spencer's mother, a wealthy heiress to a Louisiana cotton plantation, who lived in town and owned commercial property. As neighbors banded together in protest, Spencer's mother grew worried about a backlash and reached out to a local real estate broker, a Jewish woman she was acquainted with, for advice. Believing it might ease the situation for the rest of the Spencer family, who apparently do not share Richard's beliefs, the Realtor suggested to Spencer's mother that she publicly denounce her son's white supremacist views and consider selling the commercial building, earmarking a portion of the proceeds for a nonprofit fighting intolerance. Without incident, the two ended their conversation with a vague agreement to move forward to sell the property.

Then the dispute between Richard's mother and the real estate agent took a turn, and all hell broke loose.

A blog post, purportedly written by Spencer's mother, appeared online accusing the Jewish Realtor of shaking her down in the property deal.

The same week, Richard appeared on an alt-right podcast with fellow white nationalist Andrew Anglin. Before then, the two representatives of different sides of the same movement had only rarely come together.

Spencer, a tall, flamboyant, and well-dressed pseudo-intellectual, cloaks his racism in complex, difficult-to-parse logical fallacies. He holds multiple degrees from prestigious universities—the University of Virginia, the University of Chicago, and Duke—but rather than valuing those intellectually diverse environments, Spencer has leveraged his sizable knowledge and swift rhetorical skills to spin deadly hype.

Anglin, on the other hand, is a nonintellectual agitator who motivates followers more through direct calls to action than the power of covert persuasion. He openly pushes foul hate propaganda and advocates for the destruction of Jews from his popular neo-Nazi website, the Daily Stormer—a moniker he borrowed from *Der Stürmer,* a vehemently anti-Semitic publication distributed by Hitler's Third Reich.

Despite being an odd pair, Richard Spencer and Andrew Anglin developed a mutual admiration, and Anglin declared their coming together as historic for the alt-right—a forging of new alliances to bolster their cause.

Within hours of Spencer's mother allegedly publishing the critical blog, a virtual terror campaign rallied by Anglin through his website struck the unsuspecting ski town of Whitefish and its small Jewish population. Anglin started by publishing personal information and private details online about the real estate agent, her family, and other prominent Jewish residents of the Whitefish community. This questionable practice, called *doxing*, uses the web to research and publish private information about people without their permission, encouraging others to threaten and intimidate them, often with devastating results.

Unsatisfied with the fever pitch of hatred unleashed on the town, Anglin photoshopped yellow Stars of David next to the faces of four Jewish residents—including the local rabbi and her adolescent son—over a menacing image of the gates of Auschwitz. Anglin posted it online and threatened to march armed Nazis through their small downtown on the Martin Luther King Jr. holiday. When Anglin sensed the Whitefish community's fear begin to peak, he opened the floodgates for his Daily Stormer troll army to attack.

Anglin encouraged his followers to target the Realtor. "If you're in the area, maybe you should stop by and tell her in person what you think of her."

"This is Trump's America now," read one hand-scrawled letter mailed to the rabbi's home.

Another anonymous message threatened, "You deserve a bullet through your skull!"

Once the harassing phone calls and death threats began, they didn't stop. Residents installed security systems in their homes. Police stepped up patrols to look for any signs of outsiders. Local anti-hate groups, the MHRN and Love Lives Here—dubbed a "Jewish paramilitary organization" by the Daily Stormer—along with Montana governor Steve Bullock and the ADL, leaped into action when Anglin kicked a bucket of gasoline on his propaganda fire by claiming that radical "anti-Israel Islamists" would join forces with the alt-right in their armed occupation of Whitefish. "Nothing can stop us," he threatened.

Anglin's standoff never transpired, but for several weeks, his troll army dumped an avalanche of hate on peaceful Whitefish—residents, business owners, the rabbi and her family, children, peace activists, members of city government—and anyone who impeded his online blitzkrieg. The Jewish real estate agent received a call late one evening. On the other end of the line, she heard live gunshots, followed by a sinister howl.

The tiny Flathead Valley chalet of Whitefish was under siege.

I didn't know what, if anything, I could do to stop Andrew Anglin or Richard Spencer—after all, they expressed no misgivings to me about what they had done or what they believed. I didn't have a choice, though, but to find out in person and see what I could do.

Before walking over to the Whitefish auditorium for my evening talk, I sent Richard Spencer a direct message on Twitter: *Richard, I am in Whitefish. My place is overlooking your mother's building. Have a talk tonight at O'Shaughnessy Center to try to clean up your mess. Want to come?*

I didn't know Richard personally, so I gave it a shot.

The event I invited him to was a discussion at the community center about the dangers of the alt-right and specifically how the Whitefish community could best grapple with his destructive presence. As is customary in the international Jewish community on Yom HaShoah—Holocaust Remembrance Day—the local rabbi offered her blessings, and everyone settled into the theater. I became fixated on the six flickering candles burning in tribute to the six million Jewish lives extinguished for no reason other than madness. My mind wandered during the mesmerizing recital of traditional Hebrew prayer. I wondered how many in attendance lost loved ones to the same savage belief system I once condoned. *They swallowed their pain to come to hear an ex-Nazi explain to them why they're being targeted.* It filled me with sadness and shame for my past.

I spotted Richard entering the auditorium moments after the

prayers ended and the audience lights had faded to black. From my vantage point onstage, even with the glare from the spotlights in my eyes, I knew who he was. Dressed in tan slacks and a tweed sport coat, Spencer made his way up the stairs to the mezzanine and out of view from the audience. If the signature wardrobe wasn't enough of a dead giveaway, his blond Hitler Youth haircut sealed the deal.

During my presentation. I talked about my journey into and out of hate, and the movement's transition from the jackbooted extremism of thirty years ago to the subtler wave of Spencer's redux. At the end of my hour-long talk, I turned over the microphone to the audience.

After twenty minutes of thoughtful questions and heartfelt statements, I thanked those who gathered and took one final question. A long-haired, twentysomething man near the back of the auditorium rose and struggled with his words. "Mr. Picciolini," he said, his voice shaking, "thank you for coming to speak with us tonight. As you know, one of our residents is..." He cleared his throat. The audience lights remained dimmed, leaving only me aware of Spencer's presence in the upper-level balcony. The young man's voice steadied, and he continued, "One of our residents is Richard Spencer. He scares the hell out of us. So, if I may please ask, how would *you* stop him?"

I thanked the man for his question and took in a deep breath, using the moment to collect my thoughts before answering. I sympathized with the community's suffering—their pain still visible as they tried to make sense of it all.

I turned away from the man who asked me the question to gaze up from the edge of the stage toward the balcony. Spencer's crisp silhouette emerged before the shining spotlight as he leaned forward against the railing. It wrapped him with a warm halo he didn't deserve. The anxious audience followed my eyes, a hushed but building gasp escaping their lips as they realized in succession who they had shared their evening in a dark room with. Some people grabbed their belongings and shuffled toward the exits.

"How would I stop him?" I asked, repeating the man's question. I drew another breath and addressed Spencer in the balcony. "I would ask him if I could buy him a cup of coffee, and then I would tell him the conversation we'd have would be the most important one of his life. So, what do you say, Richard?"

As the event attendees hurried for the exits, it was just the two of us. I walked over to Richard, shook his hand, and thanked him for coming. I attempted to connect with him, knowing the handshake was probably as far as I would get—for the time being.

We ended up speaking for close to two hours. I did a lot of listening that night, paying close attention to his potholes. I asked about his childhood and his relationship with his father—how it felt being a dad to his own little girl and having a new son on the way. Masculinity and aggrieved entitlement are important drivers for extremists. I had a genuine interest in how it may have played into his radicalization.

Richard and I never made it for coffee that night, but over the course of our conversation I learned a lot about him. Though he was unapologetic for his behavior, I learned he became broken long before adopting his hateful beliefs. He talked about his father, who intimidated and mocked him growing up, how he'd felt crushed by his father's expectations growing up—and we talked about how, when Richard couldn't please his father, it weighed on him. I also noticed that when I asked a question that made him feel defensive, his rhetoric sharpened. When I drew back and listened, he offered insight into his cracks, perhaps unknowingly. What I heard beneath his words was not the bold demagoguery of everyone's favorite Nazi punching bag but the insecure whimpers of an insecure man pleading for attention.

Like the more extreme cases I've seen over the years, Richard gave me pause. Beneath the thin skin of even the darkest minds and the most dangerous influencers are people who long for connection and love. Unable to find it, they dig deeper holes and bury themselves in them for protection from the elements that batter them, until they unleash their frustrations on others. Richard personified the cocky, racist serial scapegoater we've come to expect. But it impressed me that he at least found the courage to come hear what I had to say about the chaos he was wreaking.

Our two hours together didn't change Richard Spencer—I didn't expect they would. But I remain inspired because we sat down together and spoke without violence or hate driving our discourse. Regardless of the lack of immediate results, several of the Seven "L" Steps of Disengagement occurred in our meeting: a *link* was established, and it may well be that link, however fragile, that leads to more opportunities to intervene; I *listened* for his potholes and heard some of them loud and clear. I made steps toward showing him he could rely on me to be open and honest, which was no small feat, but also part of the *learn* stage. If Richard ever considers an alternate path, even for one minute, in one situation, it was worth it.

"Are you into theater?" Richard asked as we left the auditorium.

"Yeah," I said. I wasn't lying. "I'm not much into musical theater, though," I added. "Maybe a punk rock opera or a stage performance of *A Clockwork Orange,* but I do enjoy seeing plays with my wife."

He pulled a colorful flyer from the community center's cork message board and held it up to show me. "Too bad," he said. "Looks like they're putting together a stage production of *Cabaret* here in the fall. My dream was always to produce a stage play." I wondered what could have been of the young playwright Richard Spencer, had racism not found him first. He caught my imagination by surprise. "I wonder if they're doing the Weimar Republic version," he said.

"Boy, I wish it would stop raining just enough for me to make a goddamn break for it," I remarked sarcastically. "Ever thought of a career change, Richard? There's still time." I smiled at him slyly, meaning what I asked—what Richard needed most was to see that another path was possible, even after all he'd done.

Though my cap provided some protection from the pouring rain, I still ended up soaked by the time I jogged the block back to my motel. I didn't care much, though. I felt a rush of optimism surging through me. I don't know why I was so hopeful, but as I unlocked the door I stood for a moment on the landing outside, turning to stare into the sky that had opened up on me. The droplets stung my eyes but I didn't glance away, noticing for the first time how low the dark clouds hung on the horizon.

Maybe I was hopeful because I've learned to love the cleansing rain—or because I know that if I could escape the storms that once pounded me, then there was hope for those still drenched by them.

# Acknowledgments

This book is my testament to how important empathy, compassion, and self-reflection are to combating hatred. Without all three, this journey would never have led me here.

Not much of anything I do is possible without the extraordinary support of a great number of people, beginning with my incredible wife, Britton, the rock with whom I've built my new life. Although I took my first steps away from extremism long before we met, you are the support I need to continue pushing forward every day. Your wisdom and rational mind are a much-appreciated ballast to my frequent risk-taking and impulse. You are my best friend, my partner, and my love, and I am forever grateful that you allowed me to be part of your life. I only hope my endless love for you offers some consolation for my many preoccupations and frequent annoyances.

Words are not enough to acknowledge my sons, Devin and Brandon, the truest catalysts for my reawakening a lifetime ago. I am beyond proud of these two fine young men. May they always remember all people are imperfect, and that through our imperfections we become part of the same family—humanity. If I impart any wisdom to them, I hope it is this: follow your dreams, and let your words and actions reflect your heart. It's okay to be vulnerable, and make sure everything you do furthers peace and promotes acceptance, caring, and equality for everyone. I love you both so much.

I must also express my gratitude and love to my parents, Anna and Enzo Picciolini. I owe them both so much for refusing to turn me away when I needed them the most. Looking back, I recognize now how they sacrificed their time with me because they wanted to make a better life for me and my brother than they had. I honor and respect them for that. Thank you for doing your best and for being decent people who care and love with all their hearts.

Thanks to Zia Lina and Zio Nando—and Zia Mary, who I miss dearly—who inspire me, and whose arms I remember comforting me as a child. I also owe a great deal to my indelible memories of Nonno Michele, the grandfather I so admired as an impressionable boy. He helped build me into the person I am today. And Nonna Nancy, who will forever remain in my heart as the foundation of our family. I miss her toughness, delicious homemade meatballs, and her constant concern for my untied shoelaces.

To my best pal and creative partner, Mike Racanelli, and my dear friend Nora Flanagan, thank you for being there through thick and thin and all the messed-up craziness in between.

Mr. Johnny Holmes, thank you for teaching me how to seek forgiveness from others and to also forgive myself. The compassion you showed me, a teenage skinhead who everyone (myself included) thought would end up dead or in prison, kept me alive and gave me hope when I wasn't sure of who I was or where to look to find myself. I owe you more than I could ever repay.

Malcolm Nance, what can I say? You are an American badass. Your words of support, your commitment to America, and your insight in this good fight, are immense. I think it's fair to say that only my friend Sarah Silverman is cooler than you. Sarah, thank you for your beautiful soul, your friendship, and for being a compassionate human being. You've made me laugh and smile through some of life's most difficult moments.

Much gratitude to all those involved in helping bring my mission to the television screen with MSNBC's *Breaking Hate* series, including the documentary film team at Part2 Pictures—David Shadrack-Smith, Amy Bucher, Eric Strauss, Chelsea Hoffman, Jon Myers, Brittany

Dowd, Aaron Chandler, Spencer Smith, Honor Maxfield, Nate Cohen, Kristen Wendell, and all the other kind and talented people who worked or appeared on the documentary series; and to my MSNBC champions Nina Weinstein and Janet Klein, thank you so much for your faith in my abilities and judgment.

I must not forget my incredible tattoo artist and friend, Pete Krol, at Krol Body Art in Chicago, for the endless hours of ink therapy—a work-life balance thing I highly recommend.

To my friend and freelance editor, Michael Mohr, your invaluable insight, and your encouragement every time I threw my exhausted hands up, pushed me to become a better writer and a better person. You taught me long ago to "kill my darlings" and to fall in love with the art of writing. Thank you also to my puzzle-solving partner, Nancy Hill. Alysha Haran, bless your skillful and artful grasp of the English language, which I don't always *got*. Much love for helping me get across the finish line.

My sincerest gratitude to the incredible team at Hachette Books— especially my editor extraordinaire, David Lamb, and my publisher, Susan Weinberg—along with my agents, Mark Falkin at Falkin Literary, Sean Berard at APA Agency, and Michael Smallbone, Kylie Dailey, and Kristy List at First Class Talent, for always believing in me and my lofty projects and crazy ideas.

My lovely, tough-as-nails colleague, Shannon Martinez, deserves big thanks for being my cheerleader, my friend, and a fellow peace warrior. To Jamie Miller, my amazing project manager and assistant, thank you for keeping me sane and alive. I believe it's working.

To all my supporters and friends who always encourage me to continue fighting the good fight, I could have accomplished none of this without you. Thank you for energizing me every single day.

My deepest gratitude to all those who have stood with me through all the twists and turns, my potholes, and the costly realizations that are necessary to do the work I am doing today. I could not have accomplished this without you.

Sincere thanks and respect goes out to the scores of true American patriots who defend the promise of our great democracy day in and day out, who stop at nothing to bring equality and justice to fruition, and who speak truth to power despite the consequences. This is just the beginning; stay the course. You have allies.

To all the former extremists around the world, much love and respect to you for proving that empathy, compassion, and forgiveness are the most valuable gifts we can give one another. Continue to stay strong, be cautiously vulnerable, and make good happen.

Last in mention but always first in my heart, this book is for my brother Alex—"Buddy." My greatest regret in life is not being there for you when you needed me. Though I still suffer your loss, your spirit carries me every day. And your passing showed me that life is something to respect, cherish, and remember—and never take for granted—no matter how dark some days appear. We have not been the same since you left us.

# Appendix I

---

# Resources and Support

In an emergency, or if you believe a credible threat of harm exists, please call your local or state police immediately by dialing 911, or contact federal authorities.

**FBI Tip Line**
Phone: +1 800-CALL-FBI (225-5324)
Website: www.fbi.gov/tips

Here are some additional crisis and intervention resources:

**Free Radicals Project**
*If you or someone you know is stuck inside the dark world of hate, the Free Radicals Project can help.*
Website: www.freeradicals.org
Contact: help@freeradicals.org

**Crisis Text Line**
Free, 24-7 text-message support from trained crisis counselors from anywhere in the United States.
Text: 741741
Website: www.crisistextline.org

**National Suicide Prevention Lifeline**

Free, 24-7 support from trained suicide prevention specialists.

Call: +1 800-273-8255 (*English*); +1 888-628-9454 (*Español*); or +1 800-799-4889 (*deaf / hard of hearing*)

Chat with a crisis counselor: www.suicidepreventionlifeline.org/chat

# Appendix II

---

# Recommended Further Reading

Arie W. Kruglanski, Jocelyn J. Bélanger, and Rohan Gunaratna, *The Three Pillars of Radicalization: Needs, Narratives, and Networks* (Oxford, UK: Oxford University Press, 2019).

Clint Watts, *Messing with the Enemy: Surviving in a Social Media World of Hackers, Terrorists, Russians, and Fake News* (New York: HarperCollins, 2018).

Eli Saslow, *Rising Out of Hatred: The Awakening of a Former White Nationalist* (New York: Doubleday, 2018).

Eric Hoffer, *The True Believer: Thoughts on the Nature of Mass Movements* (New York: Harper and Row, 1951).

Ibram X. Kendi, *How to Be an Antiracist* (New York: One World, 2019).

J. M. Berger, *Extremism* (Cambridge, MA: MIT Press, 2018).

Jeff Victoroff and Arie W. Kruglanski, eds., *Psychology of Terrorism: Classic and Contemporary Insights* (New York: Psychology Press, 2009).

John Horgan, *Walking Away from Terrorism: Accounts of Disengagement from Radical and Extremist Movements* (London: Routledge, 2009).

Kathleen Belew, *Bring the War Home: The White Power Movement and Paramilitary America* (Cambridge, MA: Harvard University Press, 2018).

Malcolm Nance, *The Plot to Destroy Democracy: How Putin and His Spies Are Undermining America and Dismantling the West* (New York: Hachette, 2018).

Michael Kimmel, *Healing from Hate: How Young Men Get Into—And Out of—Violent Extremism* (Oakland: University of California Press, 2018).

Vegas Tenold, *Everything You Love Will Burn: Inside the Rebirth of White Nationalism in America* (New York: Nation Books, 2018).

# About the Author

*Christian Picciolini* is an Emmy Award–winning producer, a renowned counter-extremism expert, a noted public speaker, husband and father, a former extremist, peace advocate, author, and hate breaker.

After denouncing the violent hate movement he was part of during his youth, Christian took on the painstaking process of making amends and rebuilding his life. While working for IBM, he earned a degree from DePaul University and later launched a global counter-extremism media and consulting firm. He has worked as an adjunct instructor at the college level and as the executive producer for *JBTV*—America's longest-running music television program.

Christian now leads the Free Radicals Project, a global radicalization prevention network committed to helping people around the world disengage from violence-based extremism. In 2018, in partnership with MSNBC and Part2 Pictures, Christian debuted *Breaking Hate,* a three-part documentary television series highlighting his anti-hate efforts.

He has briefed White House staff and the National Security Council, testified before the United States Congress, worked abroad with the State Department, trained Homeland Security officers and FBI special agents, and spoken to distinguished audiences around the world, including cadets at West Point, ambassadors at the United Nations in New York and Switzerland, royalty in Singapore, and from the TEDx stage in Denver, Colorado. Christian has helped hundreds of people disengage from extremism.

A seeker by nature, Christian's personal mantra is borrowed from Hannibal: *inveniam viam aut faciam*—"find a way or make one."